D1051299

PRAISE FOR *Lunch Money*

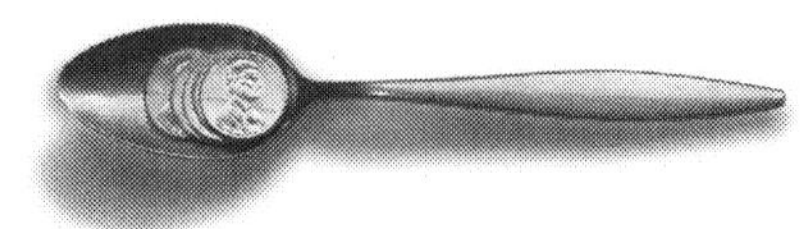

"Kate Adamick is my go-to guru for tough-minded practical advice about school food. *Lunch Money* explains why. It offers brilliant ideas for producing healthy and tasty meals while saving heaps of money on nonessentials. This book is a must for anyone who works with school food as well as parents who care what their kids eat in school."

– **MARION NESTLE**, Professor of Nutrition, Food Studies, and Public Health at New York University and author of *What to Eat* and *Food Politics*

"Ever since childhood obesity put improving the quality of school food on the national agenda, the conventional wisdom has been that fresh preparation on site – "scratch cooking" – is too expensive to consider. In this remarkable book, Kate Adamick has effectively retired that myth. Sharpen your pencils and sit down with *Lunch Money*. You will be amazed at the potential savings lurking in unexpected corners of the cafeteria, savings you can invest in the equipment and staff time needed to restore cooking to its rightful place in our children's schools. Every food service director and school food reformer in America should read this book."

– **JANET POPPENDIECK**, Professor of Sociology, Hunter College (CUNY), and author of *Free for All: Fixing School Food in America*

"With her intimate knowledge of the system, Kate Adamick demonstrates that the solutions to the school lunch issue can be tackled by regular people, as long as we have the will to change."

– **MARK BITTMAN**, *New York Times* columnist and author of *How to Cook Everything*

"I love what Kate does in her brilliant work. She's a true ambassador for sustainable change that can be achieved if people really want it. She's inspirational, no-nonsense and realistic."

– **JAMIE OLIVER**, Chef, author, and founder of *Jamie Oliver's Food Revolution*

PRAISE FOR *Lunch Money*

"As a School Nutrition Director who was very reluctant to embrace new lunch reform ideas, I was pleasantly surprised by how effective the tools in *Lunch Money* are, and how they could be applied to my own district's lunch program. Empowered by what I learned, I immediately began to implement changes in the areas of procurement of USDA commodities, reformed our menus, and implemented culinary training for all staff. The lunch money lessons learned enabled our school nutrition program to move forward from 90% processed menu items to 90% scratch cooking within 2 years and, most important, we are operating at a net profit. Once we thought we could, we were right."

– **KATHY DELTONTO**, RE-1J Nutrition Service Director, Montrose, Colorado

"*Lunch Money* answers the daunting question of how to get healthy food within hands-reach of America's public school students at an affordable price and elevates the status of the 'lunch lady' to the *Lunch Teacher*™ – those hardworking education support professionals pushing school food reform. Solid and informative, this is a must read. Well done, Chef Kate!"

– **DENNIS VAN ROEKEL**, President, National Education Association

"Adamick proves that with a few smart choices, school food service managers don't have to choose between healthy kids and a healthy bottom line."

– **CURT ELLIS**, Executive Director, FoodCorps, and Filmmaker, *King Corn*

"Chef Kate Adamick will inspire, empower and awaken your food service professionals. Her belief that school food is not the problem, but the solution, is the right step, in the right direction, at the right time. Ladies and gentlemen, start your engines! *Lunch Money* is your fuel."

– **DONNA WEST**, Child Nutrition Manager, Brownwood Elementary, Scottsboro, Alabama

LUNCH Money

SERVING HEALTHY SCHOOL FOOD IN A SICK ECONOMY

Kate Adamick

Published by Cook for America®
An imprint of Food Systems Solutions® LLC
New York, New York

Lunch Money: Serving Healthy School Food in a Sick Economy by Kate Adamick
FIRST EDITION
Book design by Greg Crawford www.gregoryguy.com
Library of Congress Cataloging-in-Publication Data has been applied for.
ISBN-10: 0984872213
ISBN-13: 978-0-9848722-1-3

Funded in part by Children's Health Foundation, to which a portion of the proceeds
from the sale of this book will be donated.

DEDICATION

Dedicated with the greatest of respect

to the Lunch Teachers™ *who serve,*

and the children they serve.

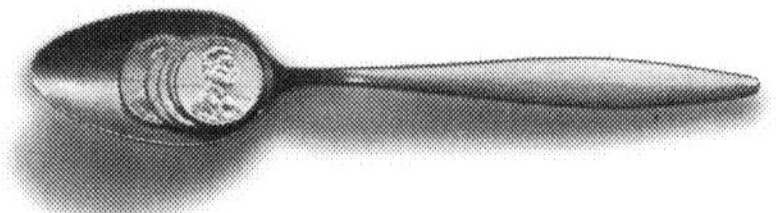

TABLE OF CONTENTS

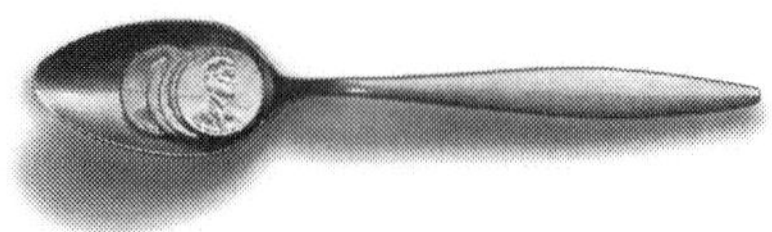

ACKNOWLEDGEMENTS

G. K. Chesterton once described gratitude as "happiness doubled by wonder." Indeed, it is with both happiness and wonder that I reflect on my path to completing this book, and it is with the greatest of gratitude that I acknowledge the following people and organizations for the vital roles they have played in its evolution.

First and foremost, my treasured "forks": Andrea Martin, David Avalos, Pam Davis, and Risa Sackman, without whom *Cook for America®* would live only in my imagination and with whom work is play. Mardell Burkholder, the wise and determined Executive Director of Children's Health Foundation, who has encouraged me for years to put on paper what has long resided only between my ears. Melissa Gibson at the Colorado Association of School Executives, who tirelessly works to ensure that teaching is learning. Antony Chiang, Sarah Smith, and Dave Luhn at the Empire Health Foundation, and Lisa Richter at GPS Capital Partners LLC, who understand and value the role of social enterprise in successful social reform. My friend Jean Hamerman, whose personal commitment to community service opened the first door for me in the world of food systems. My friend Shirley Nannini, who selflessly encouraged me to set aside my law career and pursue my joy of cooking. My long-time accountant, Stephen Zwiebel, for whom common sense and a sense of humor add up perfectly every time. My wise counsel, Margaret Ferguson, Esq., and Sherry Jetter, Esq., who handle challenging issues with grace and ingenuity. The relentlessly optimistic Jayni Chase, a bundle of positive energy who believed in me even before she had reason to. The one and only Merryl Brown, my mishpocheh through thick and thin. My beloved surrogate parents, Jim Friedman, and Brian and Joanne Rapp, whose insight, counsel, and wit keep me both grounded and reaching for the stars. And my remarkable wife, Kathryn Elizabeth Diaz, whose brilliance is outshone only by her love for me, and without whom this book – and my life – would be an unedited mess.

A NOTE FROM THE AUTHOR

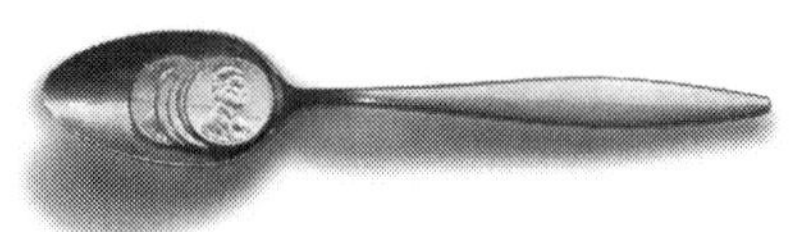

When I began my journey into the world of school food reform nearly a decade ago, I brought with me two fervent beliefs. First was the conviction that reversing dangerously escalating childhood obesity rates would require schools to return to preparing scratch-cooked meals using fresh whole foods, a belief I hold even more firmly today. The second was the opinion that successful school food reform would require substantial additional government funding for healthier foods. I soon came to believe, however, that neither our nation's economy nor its political will would be up to the task.

It was then that I began working closely with school districts to examine their day-to-day operations with an eye toward understanding how scratch cooking could be financially feasible within the existing structures and systems of the school district budget. Through years of assessment and analysis, it became clear that most school districts have two existing internal sources of revenue of which most are unaware: wasted time and wasted money.

Lunch Money: Serving Healthy School Food in a Sick Economy is the result of seven years of observation and implementation, side-by-side with committed food service directors, in both school meal preparation and service, during which we learned together that a penny saved is far more than a penny earned.

Kate Adamick
January 2012

Entrée

PART I

ENTRÉE

Lunch Money

Entrée

WHY SHOULD I READ THIS BOOK?

Over the last five years, most Americans have begun to realize that we can't continue to feed ourselves and our children as we have for the past three decades without suffering the dire consequences of diet-related illness, which is fast becoming the leading cause of death in the United States. To address the unique food-related problems facing our children, school gardens and farm-to-school programs have become more common, salad bars make regular appearances in many schools, and the topic of school food as a factor in children's health has become dinner table conversation across the country, even in the White House.

But despite all of the progress that has been made in the arena of school food reform in recent years, one factor has remained unchanged: the common belief that preparing scratch-cooked meals from fresh, whole foods is cost prohibitive.

The intent behind *Lunch Money* is to dispel this belief as mere myth. While not all of the tricks and tools presented here will apply to all school districts, every district should be able to identify at least one strategy to increase the revenue, or decrease the expenses, of its own school food service department. Those additional financial resources will then be available to pay for the staff training, kitchen equipment, local produce, and sustainably-raised meat and dairy products necessary to feed students in a healthful and responsible manner.

The goal of *Lunch Money* is to present some common solutions for saving money in your school food service operations, and to provide you with the mathematical tools to calculate the financial advantage of those solutions in your own district. The exact amount of money that can be generated by following the strategies in *Lunch Money* will depend on many factors, including the size of your district, the percentage of your students who are eligible for free or reduced meals, the prevailing market rate of labor and food in your region, and your current operating practices. And, of course, there are undoubtedly many other creative ways that you yourself may identify for improving both the bottom line of – and the food served by – your own school food service department.

As you proceed on your journey through *Lunch Money*, remember that the time you invest here could add years to the lives of the children who eat in your school district every day.

BUT SCHOOL FOOD ISN'T REALLY THAT BAD, IS IT?

If you're not convinced that your district's current school food warrants the time you will invest in reading *Lunch Money*, consider asking yourself the following questions:

1. *Are the foods served in my district's cafeteria aglow with colors not found in nature?* A cafeteria should be filled with color. But the colors should remind you of a farmers market in August, not a box of neon crayons. If a product is day-glo blue or a similar psychedelic hue, it probably originated in a chemistry lab, not on a farm.
2. *Does the cafeteria smell like a cheap diner?* If the aroma of stale fryer grease lingers in the air, you can be sure that french fries, popcorn chicken, and onion rings can't be far away. A cafeteria should smell like Grandma's kitchen on a holiday, not like a fast food chain. Deep fryers have no place in a school cafeteria.

3. *Did I take a wrong turn and end up at a professional sports arena?* School is not a once-a-year outing to a big league sporting event. Your child doesn't need to choose among hot dogs, burgers, pizza, and nachos every day. Only one of those items should be available at a time, and generally not more than once or twice a month for each.

4. *If I melt down the cans from which the food came, will I have enough metal to build a small submarine?* Food doesn't grow in cans, and shouldn't be served from them. Fruits and vegetables should be fresh and, whenever possible, local and seasonal.

5. *Is the chicken masquerading as a dinosaur?* Chickens don't have fingers. Nor do they grow in the shape of dinosaurs, dolphins, or stars. The food industry likes us to think that children will only eat poultry in cute little shapes so that it can lower production costs with cheap soy and vegetable fillers, not to mention chemical preservatives, transfats, and high fructose corn syrup.

6. *Gee, am I in the science lab?* Real food doesn't come with labels requiring a PhD in chemistry to decipher. Believe it or not, it's possible to operate a cafeteria in which there are no labels other than on the side of the milk cartons. The more time you spend "reading your food," the less likely it is to be real food.

7. *Why do the snack foods for sale remind me of my favorite Super Bowl commercials?* Children eat enough chips, candy, cookies, doughnuts, and artificially sweetened and flavored beverages during the week. Schools shouldn't be tempting kids to spend their lunch money on those items every day in the cafeteria. Fresh fruit and vegetables make perfectly good snacks.

8. *Would I be able to see the bread in a blizzard?* White is the preferred color for snow, but not such a great color for bread. There's truth in the harsh old saw, "The whiter the bread, the sooner you're dead." Beware, too, of the spongy brown stuff that's been colored with molasses and filled with high fructose corn syrup designed to trick you into thinking it is good for you. Bread should be various shades of tan, and come in different shapes and sizes, with chewy, flavorful crusts and visible whole grains and seeds.

9. *Are all these colorful toucans and leprechauns running for student body president?* Real food doesn't come tattooed with cartoon characters. When adorably animated personalities are promoting products the way pushers peddle drugs, the food industry is misusing the marketplace by exploiting your children.

10. *Are the beverages the kind favored by long distance truck drivers, night watchmen, and global securities traders?* Kids don't need a caffeine-induced jolt, boost, or buzz to get through their day. They need balanced meals made with fresh, whole foods prepared in healthful ways to keep their blood sugar levels even and their energy levels high. Caffeine is addictive. Canned and bottled beverages, coffee, and tea should all be caffeine-free.

YEAH, BUT WHAT ABOUT . . . ?

"Yeah, buts," "if onlys," and "what ifs" have come to dominate our collective consciousness as we grow increasingly disconnected and disillusioned with the notion that we can make a positive impact on our world. In a challenged and fatigued society filled with terrorist threats, corporate and government lay-offs, fiscal crises, and single-parent homes, our collective sense of insecurity has become so pervasive that it seems to cripple many efforts – at all levels of the school food chain – to create a healthier school food environment for our children.

Fearing unfavorable reports from Wall Street market analysts, many food industry executives continue to flood the marketplace with unhealthy products. Fearing the loss of campaign contributions from food processors and manufacturers, many elected officials soften their position on child advertising restrictions. Fearing unpopularity with teachers, many principals look the other way when candy is used to reward good performance and behavior by students. And fearing backlash from angry students, many school administrators do little more than pay lip service to the need for improving school food.

All of this anxiety – however legitimate or imagined – has led many of us to throw up our hands at times in frustration and exclaim, "I feel so helpless." Indeed, it's difficult not to feel helpless when confronted with so many obstacles to successful school food reform. But just as the fear of falling didn't keep any of us from learning to walk, neither can we allow our current fears to keep us from persisting in our efforts to provide our children with school food that enhances their wellness rather than compromises their health.

As adults, we have been entrusted with nurturing and caring for the next generation and, while it is certainly terrifying at times and inconvenient at others, we have a responsibility to our children to do what is in their best long-term interest. We owe it to our children to do everything possible to reduce their nearly 40% risk of acquiring Type II Diabetes. We owe it to our children to do whatever it takes to restore their life expectancy to at least our own. We owe it to our children to overcome our anxieties and sense of helplessness.

OKAY, OKAY. I GET IT. WHAT DO I NEED BEFORE I BEGIN?

In professional kitchens, chefs use one French phrase more than any other: *mise en place*. Literally, *mise en place* means "to put in place"; more generally, it means to gather all of your tools and ingredients before you begin your work.

Before beginning your work in *Lunch Money*, you should *mise en place* the following:

NECESSARY EQUIPMENT

- Two or more sharpened pencils
- Paper
- Calculator
- Your most recent food product invoices and price catalogs
- A "Do Not Disturb" sign for your door
- A beverage of your choice

A CREATIVE MIND

And remember, every school district needs to set its own path to school food reform. There is no single recipe for success. By using the worksheets and techniques in *Lunch Money*, you can begin to map out your long-term strategy by identifying a few steps that will immediately improve both the quality of your school food and your food service department's bottom line.

A POSITIVE ATTITUDE

Finally, approach your work in *Lunch Money* with a positive attitude. As Henry Ford said, "Whether you think you can or think you can't, you're right."

All That Matters

PART II

All That Matters

Twenty-first century educators have been burdened with obligations and conditions unimagined by previous generations. School days and years grow shorter while expectations and demands grow larger. The growth in federal and state testing requirements is outpaced only by cuts to federal and state funding for education.

Within the modern paradigm of public school education, duties once considered strictly part of the family domain have now been thrust upon school district administrators. Among these responsibilities is that of feeding our children through the school meals program.

Over 30,000,000 children are fed at least one government-subsidized meal a day in American schools. Frequently – and in full compliance with governing laws and regulations – those school meals consist of processed meat products, canned fruits and vegetables, flavored milk, and refined white flour. Simultaneously, we are warned by medical experts that our children face unprecedented rates of diet-related illness and, as a result, may have shorter life expectancies than our own.

Denying the existence of the crisis is no longer an option. Nor is failing to respond to it.

Food Matters

For decades, the idea that we deserved a break today – and every day – was not to be questioned, and convenience became the lynchpin of nearly every decision we made regarding our meals, including those served in schools. Sadly, today we are faced with overwhelming evidence that our quest for convenience is compromising the health and wellbeing of our most precious resource – our children.

The National Institutes of Health has stated that, of the six leading causes of death in the United States, four are linked to unhealthy diets.[1] Further, exposure to food additives and artificial colors has been linked to such conditions as ADD and ADHD,[2] and recent studies also show that one-third to one-half of all high-fructose corn syrup sampled contained unacceptable levels of mercury.[3]

The Centers for Disease Control and Prevention has stated that more than a third of today's 10-year-olds (and as many as half in minority communities) will develop Type 2 diabetes in their lifetimes,[4] and the *New England Journal of Medicine* has reported that today's children may have shorter life expectancies than their parents due to diet-related illness.[5]

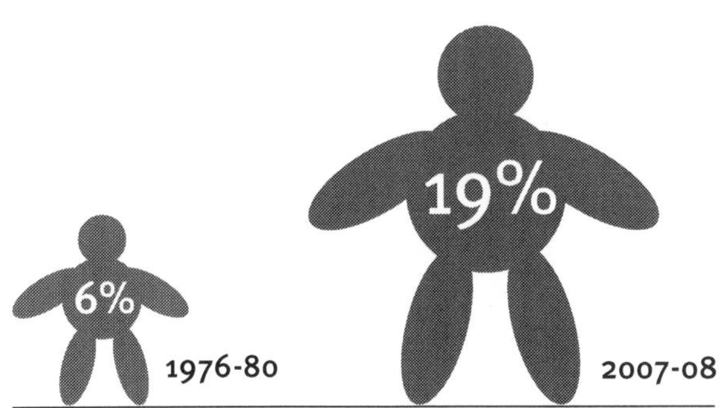

CHILDHOOD
OBESITY RATES

Obesity rates have doubled in children and more than tripled in adolescents over the last three decades,[6] and only 2% of America's children eat a healthy diet.[7] The American Medical Association has reported that blood pressure has increased over the past decade in children and adolescents, in part because of increasing numbers of overweight and obese children.[8]

The *New England Journal of Medicine* has also reported that obese children tend to be socially isolated and have high rates of eating disorders, anxiety, and depression, and that, when they reach adulthood, they are less likely than their thinner counterparts to complete college and are more likely to live in poverty.[9]

Other studies show that the more overweight a child, the more likely he or she is to be absent from school,[10] and that overweight or obese children have poorer academic outcomes.[11]

The time for allowing expediency to usurp common sense is over. The time has come to acknowledge that, in the battle for the health of our children, food matters.

Student Matters

One of the biggest myths in the school food reform movement is that if we cook healthier food "the kids won't eat it." If schools had a dime for every time those words were uttered within their hallowed halls, the dimes alone could probably fund their new healthy meal programs.

The happy reality is that most students are proud when their schools serve healthy, scratch-cooked meals. Kids are delighted to make their own selections from salad bars overflowing with fresh produce, and can be heard in cafeteria lines shouting, "Chicken with bones! I *love* chicken with bones!"

Of course, it is also true that some children will never eat anything new. Sometimes so-called "fussy eaters" are simply exerting control and sometimes their sensitive pallets have not yet become accustomed to taste sensations more familiar to adults. Regardless, it's important to remember that children are sent to school to learn. And they don't stop learning just because it's lunchtime. What and how students are fed at school teaches them how to think about food, what to think of as food, and how to behave while consuming it – all lessons they will carry with them for the remainder of their lives.

Nevertheless, though teachers and administrators struggle to comply with increasingly rigorous state testing standards, and while parents and children agonize over academic performance, far less attention is being given to school food. In fact, most school cafeterias create an environment in which students regularly learn that unhealthy food is not only acceptable, but is actually desirable.

Why do responsible, and even overprotective, adults place children directly in harm's way in the cafeteria when great care is habitually taken to avoid danger elsewhere on school grounds? Do coaches give kids the choice between playing in the gymnasium and playing in traffic? Do principals put beer kegs next to the water fountains in the school hallways? Do teachers allow teens in English class to read pornography magazines in lieu of the classics? Why, then, do we feed our children over-processed, chemical imitations of real food that, over time, can lead to serious illness and premature death?

The cause of this dangerous paradigm in America can be traced back to a confluence of events in the 1970s that started the ball rolling in the wrong direction: the nation was struggling through a recession, food prices were soaring, federal commodity crop subsidies were changing, and fast food chains – and their accompanying full-color television ads – were becoming ubiquitous. As a result, the perception – and ultimately, the definition – of food changed for most Americans. With the USDA in the untenable position of serving two masters – the food manufacturing industry and the children who are fed through the National School Lunch Program – it wasn't long before school meals became little more than processed food-like substances wrapped in space-age packaging decorated with popular cartoon characters and purporting to be "new," "improved," and "better for you." With so much external pressure to embrace mindless eating, it's no wonder that many of us are reluctant to fight the battles with our children over how they're fed.

RELISHING THE RADISH

My first childhood food memory isn't a dazzling birthday cake or a melting ice cream cone, as one might expect. Rather, it's a small blue bowl of bright red radishes.

When I was growing up, my grandfather ate radishes at every summer supper. As a devoted five-year-old who wanted to be just like him, I tenaciously set out to do the same. That year, I began to mimic his every move as he methodically reached for a newly stemmed radish, dipped it gently into sprinkled salt, and unceremoniously popped it into his mouth. I'd sit at the table next to him and unconvincingly exclaim, "Mmmmmmmm! These are good!" even as my mouth burned and tears ran down my face. If eating them would make me more like Gramps, I would happily endure the pain.

Within a few days, my grandmother asked me if I'd help her as she washed the dirt from that evening's radish crop. I vividly recall my pride at being entrusted with such an adult responsibility as I pulled the step-stool from the utility closet and dragged it to the sink for my first experience in meal preparation. My grandmother stood by my side praising my "cooking" skills and telling me that my efforts would mean the world to Gramps. As my grandmother had predicted, Gramp's face beamed when I presented him with my work, and the feeling I experienced that day of delighting others with food has never left me.

My childhood relationship with the radish evolved still further when I returned home later that summer and excitedly told my mom of my new favorite food. She promptly bought a package of radish seeds and helped me plant them in the foot-wide flower bed between the house and driveway. As I watched over the tiny plants during the next few weeks, I learned not only of their need for water, sun, and weeding, but of my own intimate connection with my planet and my food. The simple radish taught me to appreciate the fundamental links between growing, cooking, and eating.

Today, more than 40 years later, our nation's children seem to have fewer opportunities for such personal contact with their food. Instead, most of their food mysteriously arrives in sterile stores encased in flashy packages bearing a laundry list of unpronounceable ingredients, most of which have been "grown" in corporate science labs. Their contents have been freeze-dried, pre-cooked, concentrated, and vacuum-packed. And even the whole foods they consume have often been genetically modified, sprayed with myriad pesticides, or derived from animals injected with a virtual pharmacy of antibiotics and hormones.

Our children now live in a world in which more than 25% of their meals are eaten in front of a television set and another 25% in the car. Fully one-third of American children eat in fast food chains every day. Under such circumstances, rarely do children learn that meals are an opportunity for leisure, conversation, and hospitality. Rather, millions of media message each year scream out to them that food is about convenience, image, and instant gratification.

But there is hope. In recent years, I have had the good fortune to observe a classroom full of six-year olds shout "Me! Me! Me!" when asked who wanted more of the beans they had just sautéed together as a group, to hear an eight-year-old exclaim, "It has veins just like I do!" when examining a leafy collard green under a magnifying glass, and to witness a teenager utter in amazement, "It's magic!" after pulling a carrot from the ground.

But while certainly magical, these children's experiences are hardly magic. Rather, they are nothing more than opportunities diligently discovered and passionately pursued. With a little imagination and initiative, classrooms become make-shift kitchens, city balconies become urban vegetable gardens, family field trips become agricultural adventures to farmer's markets and farms, and narrow suburban flower beds become miniature patches of radishes.

Unfortunately, in our never-ending efforts to give our children more of what we think they want, our frenzied schedules often prevent us from providing them with more of what they really need. As a result, we all too quickly fall into the habit of picking up ready-to-eat meals on the way home from work or stopping for burgers on the way home from soccer practice. But as adults, the responsibility for shepherding our youth through the perils of our modern industrialized society, and reconnecting them to their own roots in the natural world, rests squarely and unequivocally on our shoulders. Perhaps the best way to accomplish this overwhelming task is by exposing our children to food in ways that not only feed their growing bodies, but nurture their very souls. Perhaps the best way is by teaching our children to relish the radish.

Money Matters

While few educators deny the need for meaningful school food reform, most struggle to understand how they can afford to replace their existing processed convenience foods with healthier cooked-from-scratch meals.

Lunch Money is designed to answer your questions by providing you with new strategies for decreasing expenses and increasing revenues associated with your school district's school meals program. With this knowledge and these computational tools in your financial arsenal, you will be armed to feed your students' bodies in a manner that will better enable you to nourish their minds.

For most Americans, math is intimidating. Perhaps for no reason beyond the fact that they missed a day of school in the second grade and felt as if they never caught up, many Americans will avoid math like the plague. Unfortunately, their fear is not baseless. In the Organization for Economic Cooperation & Development's 2009 Program for International Student Assessment, fifteen-year-olds in the United States ranked 25th among their peers in 34 countries in math.

Yet the routine use of simple mathematical formulas is critical to successful budget management. The use of math in the school food world can transform the old adage, "A penny saved, is a penny earned," into "A penny saved is thousands and thousands of dollars earned."

Throughout Part III of *Lunch Money*, entitled "Money Problems," you will find simple mathematical formulas and other useful tools, designed to uncloak the mysteries of funding cooked-from-scratch school meals within the confines of ever shrinking school budgets. To support each of the major concepts in Part III, you will find a series of examples and case studies that highlight specific points. Part IV, entitled "Show Me the Money," describes a fictional site visit to a school cafeteria that will allow you to test the knowledge and skills you learned in Part III. And in Part V, entitled "Tools of the Trade," you will find worksheets and guidelines for applying the formulas and problem-solving strategies in your own school or district.

EXAMPLE

A PENNY SAVED IS A PENNY EARNED

1.	Number of meals served in your district per school day		5,000
2.	Number of school days per year	x	175
3.	Number of meals served in your district per school year *(Multiply Line 1 by Line 2, above)*		875,000
4.	Multiply by a penny	x	$ .01
5.	**Total saved per year by saving one penny per meal**		**$ 8,750**

Now that you have seen how quickly pennies can add up, use the worksheet below to calculate what your savings would be once a year if you were to save one cent per meal served.

FORMULA/WORKSHEET: A PENNY SAVED IS A PENNY EARNED

1.	Number of meals served in your district per school day		______
2.	Number of school days per year	x	______
3.	Number of meals served in your district per school year *(Multiply Line 1 by Line 2, above)*		______
4.	Multiply by a penny	x	$ .01
5.	**Total saved per year by saving one penny per meal**		**$** ______

✔ **NOTE:** *The corresponding "A Penny Saved is a Penny Earned" worksheet for use in your own district can be found in Part V, Tools of the Trade, Worksheet #2.*

By using these worksheets, you will begin to identify the areas in your own school food service operation that can lead to increased revenue and decreased expenses – money that can then be used to fund scratch-cooked school meals.

This is the magic of *Lunch Money* and the key to the success of school districts around the country that have successfully made the move back to scratch cooking. Yes, local, fresh produce costs more than canned fruits and vegetables, but by identifying unnecessary expenses and capturing additional revenue, you can apply that "reclaimed money" toward better ingredients, more efficient equipment, and professional training for your staff. You *can* feed kids what they need and stay within your budget. *Lunch Money* will show you how.

Money Problems

PART III

Money Problems

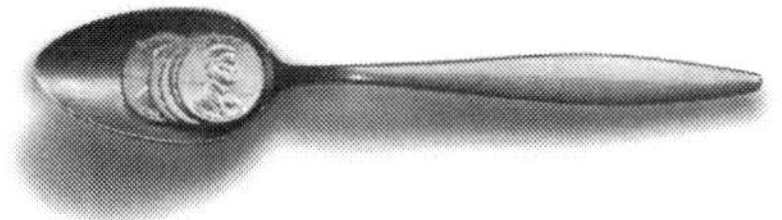

"Money, money everywhere, and not a cent to spend" is a suitable paraphrase of a familiar adage that applies to most school food service departments. That's good news for everyone who has ever given a moment's thought to meaningful school food reform. But identifying additional revenue sources and unnecessary expenses is a task that often goes undone because of the relentless demands of putting food on the trays of hundreds or thousands of hungry students – often two or more times each school day. Staff shortages, missed deliveries, class schedule changes, equipment breakdowns, and countless other challenges occupy nearly every working hour of most school food service directors who, if given the right training and tools, could turn their own departments into streamlined business operations worthy of any MBA graduate.

This section is designed to provide anyone who is serious about returning to scratch-cooked school meals with the tools necessary to calculate the financial impact of key operational changes that will not only lead to a healthier bottom line, but will also result in healthier students. You will find examples of effective financial strategies applied to a fictional school district called "Meanswell," which operates on a 175-day, 35-week school year, and is home to a hungry group of 5,000 students. Under federal regulations governing the National School Lunch Program, 3,000 Meanswell students are eligible for free meals, 500 are eligible for reduced meals, and 1,500 are not eligible for either free or reduced meals. Note that Meanswell is located in a state that does not provide additional funding for school meals and, as a result, it receives only federal funding. With any luck, your district is located in a state that supplements the federal funding for school meals. If so, remember to take state reimbursements into account when running your own calculations.

By studying these examples and using the blank worksheets contained in *Part V: Tools of the Trade*, you will be well equipped to begin transforming school food in your own district from a problem into a solution.

A FEW FACTS ABOUT THE FEDERAL SCHOOL MEALS PROGRAM

Understanding some of the key concepts inherent in working with the federal school meals program will enable you to better utilize the mathematical formulas and financial strategies in *Lunch Money.*

PARTICIPATION IN THE FEDERAL MEALS PROGRAM

Both public and non-profit private schools serving students in grades 12 and below are eligible to participate in the federally subsidized school meals program. Districts and schools that choose to participate get federal cash subsidies and USDA commodity foods for each breakfast and lunch they serve that meets federal requirements, provided free or reduced price meals are offered to eligible students.

FREE, REDUCED & PAID CLASSIFICATIONS

The amount of federal cash reimbursements provided to a school district for serving school breakfast and lunch is determined by classifying students into three categories based on their family income. The categories are free, reduced, and paid:

FREE: *Children from families with incomes at or below 130 percent of the poverty level are eligible for free meals.*

REDUCED: *Children from families with incomes above 130 percent, but at or below 185 percent, of the poverty level are eligible for reduced-price meals, for which students can be charged no more than 40 cents for lunch or 30 cents for breakfast.*

PAID: *Children from families with incomes over 185 percent of the poverty level may be charged full price for breakfast and lunch, though their meals are still subsidized by the federal government to some extent. School districts set their own prices for paid (sometimes called "full price") meals.*

REIMBURSEABLE MEALS

Historically, school districts have been able to meet any one of several meal patterns to qualify for federal cash reimbursement for school meals. Under USDA regulations slated to become effective as early as the 2012–2013 school year, the system will be simplified by requiring all districts to comply with a single meal pattern, called the "food-based system."

In order to qualify for federal cash reimbursement for meals, all schools will be required to offer each of the following five components, in regulated age-appropriate portion sizes, from which students must actually take three components, including fruit or vegetable. This system is known as "Offer versus Serve":*

- *Meat and meat alternative options, for example, legumes, cheese, nuts, yogurt*
- *Grains*
- *Vegetable*
- *Fruit*
- *Fluid Milk*

**NOTE: Special rules regarding the optional offering of meat, meat alternatives, and vegetables apply at breakfast.*

In addition, school meals must meet other requirements, for example, minimum and maximum limitations on calories and restrictions on the amount and types of fat that a meal may contain.

In general, however, decisions about what specific foods to serve, and how those foods are prepared, are made by the school district and not by the federal government.

FOOD SERVICE DEPARTMENTS AS SEPARATE PROFIT & LOSS CENTERS

Each school food service department must operate as a non-profit program, separate and apart from the general funds budget of the school district. The general funds budget may be used to subsidize the food service department budget, but the food service department budget may not be used to subsidize the general funds budget, except to reimburse the district for permissible direct and indirect expenses. Thus, food service department revenues may be used to purchase a new oven for the kitchen or to reimburse the district for the electricity used in the kitchen, but may not be used to purchase blackboards for the classrooms or football uniforms.

Once upon a time, children waited all year for dessert. Many of our grandparents told happy tales of finding a precious peppermint stick tucked in their stockings on Christmas morning, to be savored slowly in anticipation of the next, which wouldn't arrive for another year.

A favorite book among children and adults alike is *Little House in the Big Woods*, by Laura Ingalls Wilder, which tells the story of a pioneer family struggling to hunt, grow, gather, and prepare its own food for a year. In the book, Ingalls Wilder describes the "little heart-shaped cakes" that she and her sister found in their Christmas stockings:

> *Over their delicate brown tops was sprinkled white sugar. The sparking grains lay like tiny drifts of snow. The cakes were too pretty to eat. Mary and Laura just looked at them. But at last Laura turned hers over, and she nibbled a tiny nibble from underneath where it wouldn't show.*

We don't have to reach too far back into our collective history to recall that dessert used to be special. Maybe there was a peppermint stick on Christmas morning, a pie on Sunday afternoons, or an ice cream cone on the Fourth of July. Unfortunately, our modern culture has taught children that snacks, treats, and desserts accompany nearly every meal, are frequently served between meals, and often serve as the meals themselves. It's no surprise that childhood obesity is rampant.

As a result, serving children dessert in schools is not only ill-advised, it is a waste of financial resources, both in terms of labor and food cost. Removing dessert items from school menus can help improve the overall quality of the meals served, as well as the food service department's bottom line. The money saved by eliminating dessert items such as cookies, brownies, ice cream, pudding, and cake, can be used to help pay for fresh fruits and vegetables and higher quality protein items. In addition, the time saved baking, wrapping, and serving such items can be used to prepare fruits and vegetables for salad bars and to cook entrées from scratch.

One of the most important lessons adults can teach a child today is that snacks and treats are not a daily entitlement. Limiting the number of times a year that dessert is served in school to such special occasions as the winter holiday party and the end-of-year celebration will serve as a teachable moment in which students will be reminded that such food items, while not forbidden, are to be eaten on special occasions, rather than as daily fare.

EXAMPLE

COST SAVINGS OF ELIMINATING DESSERT FROM THE MENU

Meanswell School District serves reimbursable lunch to an average of 5,000 students each day throughout the 35-week school year. Once a week, Meanswell serves cookies for dessert. Each child gets one cookie, which the staff bakes off in the morning from pre-shaped frozen dough. Each puck of frozen cookie dough costs 12 cents.

CALCULATING THE REAL COST OF DESSERT

STEP ONE CALCULATE THE NUMBER OF SERVINGS OF DESSERT SERVED PER SCHOOL YEAR

1. Number of servings of dessert served per day		5,000
2. Number of days per week dessert is served	x	1
3. Number of servings of dessert served per week *(Multiply line 1 by line 2, above)*		5,000
4. Number of weeks per school year that dessert is served	x	35
5. Number of Servings of Dessert Served per School Year		**175,500**

STEP TWO CALCULATE AMOUNT OF MONEY SAVED BY ELIMINATING DESSERT

6. Number of servings of dessert served per school year *(Insert from line 5, above)*		175,500
7. Food cost per serving of dessert	x	$ .12
8. Savings Per School Year by Eliminating Dessert		**$ 21,000.00**

As if this figure is not impressive enough, it is important to keep in mind that it represents a district in which dessert is being served only once per week. In schools that serve dessert twice, three times, or even more each week, the totals will be much greater.

✔ **NOTE:** *The corresponding "Sweet Dough" worksheet for use in your own district can be found in Part V, Tools of the Trade, Worksheet #3.*

MORE DOUGH: *The example above calculates only the savings related to the food cost of the dessert item. In addition to these substantial savings are other savings related to the cost of the labor time necessary to order and receive the dessert item (or the ingredients) from the distributor, inventory the items in storage, bake the items off, package or wrap the items when appropriate, set up and break down the display of the items, and wash any dishes generated in the process. There may also be additional expenses related to packaging, such as plates or portion cups for cakes and puddings, and plastic or paper bags for cookies.*

Milk Moolah

While shouting "Fire!" in a crowded theater was once thought to be the surest way to cause a riot, today one only needs to shout the words, "Chocolate milk!" in the middle of a school board meeting to see social unrest flare. Across the country, flavored milk has become the honorary lightning rod in school food reform efforts. Faced with competing claims that these sugar-laden dairy drinks are either weapons of mass destruction or the sole significant source of calcium in a child's diet, school administrators and parents alike are frequently unsure about how often – if at all – flavored milk should be served to students.

Regardless of your position on the benefits or detriments of flavored milk, the financial impact of switching to plain white, or unflavored, milk can be substantial for many districts. In some districts, the price of an 8-ounce serving of flavored milk can exceed the cost of an 8-ounce serving of unflavored milk by as much as 6 cents, although 1/2 to 2 cents per serving is more common. When the price per serving of flavored milk exceeds the price per serving of unflavored milk, it's worth the time to calculate the financial impact of the added expense over the course of a school year.

EXAMPLE

CALCULATING THE COST OF FLAVORED MILK

Meanswell School District serves flavored milk at both breakfast and lunch to an average of 5,000 students each day throughout the 35-week school year. The price for an 8-ounce carton of flavored milk is only 1/2 cent ($0.005) more than an 8-ounce carton of unflavored milk.

Given the small price differential between flavored and unflavored milk, how much money will Meanswell really save by serving only unflavored milk?

FLAVORED MILK SERVINGS

STEP ONE CALCULATE THE NUMBER OF SERVINGS OF FLAVORED MILK SERVED PER SCHOOL YEAR

1.	Average number of cartons of flavored milk served per meal period		5,000
2.	Number of times flavored milk is served per week	x	10
3.	Number of cartons of flavored milk served per week *(Multiply line 1 by line 2, above)*		50,000
4.	Number of weeks per school year that flavored milk is served	x	35
5.	**Number of Cartons of Flavored Milk Served per School Year** *(Multiply line 3 by line 4, above)*		**1,750,000**

DIFFERENCE IN COST BETWEEN FLAVORED AND UNFLAVORED MILK

STEP TWO CALCULATE THE PREMIUM PRICE PER CARTON OF FLAVORED MILK

6.	Price per case of flavored milk		$ 15.75
7.	Price per case of unflavored milk	–	$ 15.40
8.	Premium price paid per case of flavored milk *(Subtract line 7 from line 6, above)*		$ .35
9.	Number of cartons of milk per case	÷	70
10.	**Premium Price per Carton of Flavored Milk** *(Divide line 8 by line 9, above)*		**$ 0.005**

STEP THREE CALCULATE AMOUNT OF MONEY SAVED PER YEAR BY SERVING ONLY UNFLAVORED MILK

11.	Number of Cartons of Flavored Milk Served per School Year *(Insert from line 5, above)*		1,750,000
12.	Premium Price per Carton of Flavored Milk *(Insert from line 10, above)*	x	$ 0.005
13.	**Amount of Money Saved per Year by Serving Only Unflavored Milk** *(Multiply line 11 by line 12, above)*		**$ 8,750.00**

✔ **NOTE:** *The corresponding "Milk Moolah" worksheet for use in your own district can be found in Part V, Tools of the Trade, Worksheet #4.*

MORE MILK MATH . . . *Generally speaking, there are 22 to 24 grams of sugar in a typical 8-ounce serving of flavored milk; that's 10 to 12 more grams of added sugars than in a comparable serving of unflavored milk (of equal fat content). There are 4 grams of sugar per teaspoon, and approximately 115 teaspoons of sugar per pound. Thus, a child who drinks flavored milk every day for lunch consumes 1,800 to 2,160 more grams of sugar per 175-day school year than a child who drinks an equal amount of unflavored milk. That's 3.9 to 4.7* pounds *of added sugars. And, of course, children who drink flavored milk for both breakfast and lunch consume twice that amount.*

Like dessert (see "Sweet Dough," above), limiting the number of times a year that flavored milk is served, to perhaps only the winter holiday party and the end-of-year party, will create teachable moments in which students will be reminded that such food items are reserved for special occasions.

EXAMPLE

THE ADDED SUGARS IN FLAVORED MILK

Meanswell School District serves both flavored and unflavored milk at both breakfast and lunch to an average of 5,000 students each day throughout the 175-day school year. Each 8-ounce carton of unflavored milk contains 12 grams of sugar. Each 8-ounce carton of flavored milk contains 22 grams of sugar. How much added sugar is the Meanswell student body consuming each year as a result of Meanswell serving flavored milk?

ADDED SUGARS IN A SERVING OF FLAVORED MILK

STEP ONE CALCULATE THE NUMBER OF ADDED GRAMS OF SUGARS PER 8 OZ CARTON OF FLAVORED MILK

1.	Total number of grams of sugars in an 8 oz carton of flavored milk		22 g
2.	Total number of grams of sugars in an 8 oz carton of unflavored milk	–	12 g
3.	**Total number of added grams of sugars in each 8 oz carton of flavored milk** *(Subtract line 2 from line 1, above)*		**10 g**

STEP TWO CALCULATE THE NUMBER OF TEASPOONS OF ADDED SUGARS PER 8 OZ CARTON OF FLAVORED MILK

4.	Total number of added grams of sugars in each 8 oz carton of flavored milk		10 g
5.	Number of grams of sugars per teaspoon	÷	4.2 g
6.	**Total number of teaspoons of added sugars per 8 oz carton of flavored milk** *(Divide line 4 by line 5, above)*		**2.38 tsp**

ADDED SUGARS IN A YEAR'S WORTH OF FLAVORED MILK

STEP THREE CALCULATE THE NUMBER OF TEASPOONS OF ADDED SUGARS PER SCHOOL YEAR FOR A CHILD DRINKING FLAVORED MILK

7.	Total number of teaspoons of added sugars per 8 oz carton of flavored milk *(Insert total from line 6, above)*		2.38 tsp
8.	Number of school days per year	x	175
9.	Number of times per school day that flavored milk is offered	x	2
10.	**Total number of teaspoons of added sugars per school year for a child drinking flavored milk for both breakfast and lunch** *(Multiply the amounts in lines 7, 8 and 9, above)*		**833 tsp**

STEP FOUR CALCULATE THE NUMBER OF POUNDS OF ADDED SUGARS PER SCHOOL YEAR FOR A CHILD DRINKING FLAVORED MILK

11.	Total number of teaspoons of added sugars per school year for a child drinking flavored milk for both breakfast and lunch *(Insert total from line 10, above)*		833 tsp
12.	Approximate number of teaspoons of sugars per pound	÷	115 tsp
13.	**Total number of pounds of added sugars per school year for a child drinking flavored milk** *(Divide line 11 by 12, above)*		**7.24 lbs**

A FEW MORE MILK MUSINGS

KIDS WILL DRINK UNFLAVORED MILK *If your primary concern about removing flavored milk from your district continues to be the potential for decreased milk consumption by students, take this opportunity to step back and think creatively about how to increase your students' consumption of unflavored milk. Some successful ideas include adding a Breakfast in the Classroom program in which every child is provided with an 8-ounce serving of unflavored milk every morning, or scheduling recess before lunch so that students arrive in the cafeteria thirsty following a period of active play.*

OTHER HIDDEN MILK EXPENSES *Another hidden expense on your milk invoice may be found in the packaging in which your milk arrives. When milk is served in plastic bottles rather than in traditional cardboard cartons, the additional charge can be as high as 5 to 8 cents per serving. If you are currently serving milk in individual plastic bottles, do the math to figure out how much money you will save by returning to the cardboard cartons.*

And don't forget to include the cost of replacing all of those meals that end up on the floor when young students spill their entire tray in a futile effort to catch the plastic bottle of milk (with its high center of gravity) as it tumbles off the tray and through the air. It's difficult not to cry over spilled milk when you start adding up all that money.

Commodity Cash Cow

During the course of a lifetime, most of us purchase something we don't need simply because it's on sale. Maybe it's a pair of jeans that don't quite fit, a third gym bag even though we don't belong to a gym, or another set of mixing bowls just in case our thirty-year-old son ever moves out of the house and needs a set for his own apartment. We convince ourselves that the purchase is a good idea because it will save us money, when in reality we end up with both something we don't want and a smaller bank account. Once we step back and rethink our purchase, we're usually left with the empty feeling of having less rather than more.

A similarly fruitless purchasing decision is made across the country early each calendar year, when school districts that participate in the National School Lunch Program place their commodity orders for the following school year.

But before we examine how commodity ordering can make or break a school food budget, let's first review how the commodity food system works.

Federal aid for school meals comes in two forms. First, the government provides school districts with cash reimbursements to help pay for school meals served to children whose family income falls below certain economic thresholds. In addition, the United States Department of Agriculture (the "USDA") provides school districts with surplus foods through the federal commodity food program.

The list of commodity products available to schools includes raw, whole muscle meat products such as 8-piece chicken, turkey breasts, pork loins, and ground beef, ground pork, and ground turkey. While these products are almost certainly the result of the factory farming system that now passes for animal husbandry, they are nonetheless basic cuts of meat that our grandmothers would recognize as food. These "brown box" products are available to most school districts for the cost of shipping and handling – about $3 to $5 per case – and can be turned into herb-roasted chicken, barbecued pork, sliced turkey sandwiches, meatballs, or any number of other delicious scratch-cooked items.

But as a result of misleading messages from industry and industry-sponsored organizations, most school districts spend cold hard cash from their diminishing budgets to turn free commodity foods into highly processed products on the mistaken belief that (1) students prefer them, (2) food preparation will be faster, and (3) they will save money by doing so. Interestingly, our retired armed forces officials are now holding these same types of processed meats products partially responsible for our nation's lack of military readiness.[12]

According to the USDA, "at least 70 [commodity] products are reprocessed."[13] Those that are reprocessed most often are:

BASIC COMMODITY	PROCESSED END PRODUCTS
Pork	Rib-shaped patties, cooked sausage patties and links
Beef	Charbroiled patties, taco filling, meat balls
Frozen fruit	Fruit pops, turnovers
Chicken	Nuggets, patties, roasted pieces, breaded chicken
Turkey	Turkey ham, bologna, breast deli slices
Flour, mozzarella, tomato paste	Frozen pizza

The USDA also reports that as much as half[14] of the approximately one billion pounds[15] of USDA commodities made available to schools each school year are "directly diverted" for further processing.

Districts that engage in the practice of direct diversions needlessly spend thousands, tens of thousands, or even hundreds of thousands of dollars each school year to turn healthy, usable food into convenience products that are often laden with soy fillers, sugars, salt, hydrogenated oils, artificial colors, flavors, and preservatives.

How much money, exactly, do school districts spend on processing free food? It's difficult to say, although multiplying just $1.00 per pound processing fee times 500,000,000 pounds of USDA commodities comes to $500,000,000 per year. That's about 9 cents per day for each of America's nearly 32 million students who participate in the National School Lunch Program.

CALCULATING YOUR OWN COMMODITY COSTS: *To calculate how much money your own school district is spending to process commodities, simply collect all of the previous school year's invoices from the vendors to which you diverted your commodities and add up the total processing fees (less processor rebates). Most school districts are amazed to discover that the result is usually a figure in the thousands, tens of thousands, or even hundreds of thousands of dollars. Then ask yourself how your own local economy might be better served by spending that money closer to home to pay your own staff to cook the unprocessed commodities from scratch.*

If your district belongs to a purchasing co-op that requires you to process your commodities, give serious consideration to withdrawing from the co-op. If storage is an issue (because of less frequent but larger deliveries), consider sharing freezer and cooler space with nearby districts (or other large institutions such as hospitals or prisons) that may have surplus space, renting relatively inexpensive space in local warehouse facilities (sometimes located near transportation hubs such as airports), or using the money you save by not processing your commodities to invest in new walk-in coolers and freezers in your district.

EXAMPLE

SAVING MONEY BY ELIMINATING DIRECT DIVERSIONS OF COMMODITIES

Meanswell School District learns that it can directly divert its raw commodity chicken to a processor in a "fee-for-service" arrangement in which Meanswell will receive chicken nuggets for only $1.02 per pound. This represents a significant savings over the $2.25 per pound that Meanswell would pay for chicken nuggets on the open market. The reason for the savings, Meanswell is told, is that the value of the donated commodities in the chicken nuggets will not be included in the price per pound that Meanswell pays. Instead, Meanswell will only pay the $1.02 per pound processing fee, which represents the processor's costs for labor, packaging, added ingredients (including soy fillers, salt, sugar and fat), and administrative overhead. Convinced that it will save a tremendous amount of money, Meanswell diverts its commodity chicken to the processor and orders 500 cases of chicken nuggets.

When the invoice arrives, it looks like this:

PARLOUS POULTRY PROCESSORS
333 PULLET PLACE, CAPONVILLE, USA 98765
PHONE: 987.654.8855 FAX: 987.654.8877
INFO@PPP.COM

INVOICE
INVOICE # 1111
DATE: January 27, 2012

TO Meanswell School District
Attn: Food Service Director
1234 Improvin Lane
Swelltown USA 12345
654.123.4567
Customer ID ABC12345

SHIP TO Central Warehouse
Meanswell School District
4321 Storit Street
Swelltown, USA 12345
654.123.7654

SALESPERSON	JOB	SHIPPING METHOD	SHIPPING TERMS	DELIVERY DATE	PAYMENT TERMS	DUE DATE
Henrietta Peck		Ground	FOB Destination	01/25/12	Net 30	02/24/12

QTY	ITEM #	DESCRIPTION	UNIT PRICE	WEIGHT	LINE TOTAL
800 CS	666	BREADED CKN NUGGET 6/5#	30.60	24,000 LB	$24,480
			TOTAL	**24,000 LB**	**$24,480**

THANK YOU FOR YOUR BUSINESS!

Meanswell reviews the invoice and sees that it paid only $24,480 for 24,000 pounds of chicken nuggets. As a result, Meanswell happily believes that it saved $1.23 per pound, for a total of $29,520, over the price it would have paid for 24,000 pounds of those same chicken nuggets if they had been ordered directly from the distributor at $2.25 per pound.

But Meanswell didn't *save* $29,520; it *spent* $24,480. If Meanswell had elected to exercise its third option – choosing NOT to process the free commodity chicken and, instead, getting it delivered as a raw, brown box product and cooking it from scratch – Meanswell would have had the opportunity to save more money and serve healthier food to its students.

CAPITALIZING ON COMMODITIES: *The biggest savings to be realized in the commodity arena is usually by cooking the raw brown box meat products rather than diverting them to industry for processing. To maximize your commodity allotment, focus your commodity ordering on products that are the most expensive to purchase on the open market, typically raw meats and cheeses. First, order as much raw meat and block cheese products as allowed. Then, move on to fresh produce (if available), and dried and frozen fruit (such as dried cranberries and raisins, which can be used on the salad bars, and frozen blueberries and strawberries, which can be used to make compotes and smoothies).*

Bean Counting

"Beans, beans, the musical fruit, the more you eat, the more you . . ." – you know the rest. While beans, also known as "legumes," have long been the subject of adolescent humor, the truth is that they are a food staple throughout the world because they are generally high in fiber and protein, low in fat, and more affordable than most meat products. For the same reasons, they can also play a critical role in providing affordable, healthy, and delicious school meals.

Legumes are species of plants that produce fruits in the form of double-seamed pods with a single row of seeds inside. Although we sometimes eat the entire pod, as we do in the spring when we eat sugar snap peas, we more typically eat just the seeds themselves. Legume seeds come in three different shapes: flat, like lentils; kidney-shaped, like beans; and round, like peas. Some varieties commonly used by school food service departments are kidney beans, black beans, pinto beans, navy beans, garbanzo beans, and lentils.

Legumes can help reduce the cost of school meals by replacing more expensive protein items such as chicken, beef, pork, and cheese at least once a week. However, while many varieties of legumes are commonplace on school menus, they are typically procured in canned form. Because canned beans must be drained before cooking, and dried beans expand while cooking (due to the absorption of water or other liquid), switching from canned beans to dried beans can result in substantial savings over the course of a school year.

EXAMPLE

COMPARING THE COST OF CANNED BEANS TO DRY BEANS

Meanswell School District serves kidney beans as the protein component of a reimbursable lunch once a week throughout the 35-week school year to an average of 5,000 students. A case of 6 #10 cans of kidney beans costs $31.05 and yields 68 ounces of drained kidney beans per can. A 20-pound case of dried kidney beans costs $33.20 and yields 2.6 pounds of cooked kidney beans for every pound of dried kidney beans. How much money would Meanswell School District save by switching from canned kidney beans to dried kidney beans?

BEAN YIELDS CHART

VARIETY	CANNED USDA Recommended Drained Weight (Minimum in Ounces per #10 Can)	DRIED 1 Pound Raw Yields This Number of Pounds Cooked*
Garbanzo Beans	68 oz	2.2 lbs
Kidney Beans	68 oz	2.6 lbs
Pinto Beans	68 oz	2.8 lbs

* Source: *The Book of Yields: Accuracy in Food Costing and Purchasing*, by Francis T. Lynch.

CALCULATING THE COST OF CANNED KIDNEY BEANS

STEP ONE CALCULATE YIELD OF CANNED KIDNEY BEANS

1.	Drained weight per #10 can of kidney beans		68 oz
2.	Number of #10 cans per case	x	6
3.	Ounces per Case of Drained Canned Kidney Beans *(Multiply Line 1 by Line 2, above)*		408 oz

STEP TWO CALCULATE PRICE PER POUND OF CANNED KIDNEY BEANS

4.	Price per case of canned kidney beans		$ 31.05
5.	Number of ounces per case of canned kidney beans *(Insert from Line 3, above)*	÷	408 oz
6.	Price per ounce of canned kidney beans *(Divide Line 4 by Line 5, above)*		$ .077 per oz
7.	Number of ounces per pound	x	16 oz per lb
8.	**Price per Pound of Canned Kidney Beans** *(Multiply Line 6 by Line 7, above)*		**$ 1.23 per lb**

CALCULATING THE COST OF DRIED KIDNEY BEANS

STEP THREE CALCULATE YIELD OF DRIED KIDNEY BEANS

9.	Yield of 1 pound of dried kidney beans after cooking		2.6 lbs
10.	Number of pounds of dried kidney beans per case	x	20
11.	**Total Pounds of Kidney Beans per Case of Dried Beans After Cooking** *(Multiply Line 9 by Line 10, above)*		**52 lbs**

STEP FOUR CALCULATE PRICE PER POUND OF DRIED KIDNEY BEANS

12.	Price per case of dried kidney beans		$ 33.20 per case
13.	Number of pounds of kidney beans per case of dried beans after cooking *(Insert from Line 11, above)*	÷	52 lbs
14.	**Price per Pound of Cooked Dried Beans** *(Divide Line 12 by Line 13)*		**$ .64 per lb**

CALCULATING THE DIFFERENCE BETWEEN DRIED AND CANNED KIDNEY BEANS

STEP FIVE CALCULATE DIFFERENCE IN PRICE PER POUND OF CANNED BEANS VERSUS PRICE OF DRIED BEANS

15. Price per pound of canned kidney beans — $ 1.23 per lb
(Insert from Line 8, above)

16. Price per pound of cooked dried beans — – $ .64 per lb
(Insert from Line 14, above)

17. **Savings per Pound by Serving Dried Beans Versus Canned Beans** — **$ .59 saved per lb**
(Line 15 minus Line 16, above)

STEP SIX CALCULATE MONEY SAVED EACH SCHOOL YEAR BY SERVING DRIED BEANS VERSUS CANNED BEANS

18. Number of lunches served per day — 5000 servings per day

19. Number of 2 oz servings per pound of beans — ÷ 8 servings per lb

20. Number of pounds of beans needed — 625 lbs per day served
(Divide Line 18 by Line 19, above)

21. Number of school weeks per year — x 35 weeks per school year

22. Number of pounds of beans used per school year (served 1 day per week) — 21,875 lbs per school year
(Multiply Line 20 by Line 21, above)

23. Savings per pound by serving dried beans versus canned beans — x $ .59 lb saved
(Insert from Line 17, above)

24. **Savings per Year by Serving Dried Beans Versus Canned Beans** — **$ 12,906.25 saved per year**
(Multiply Line 22 by Line 23, above)

✔ **NOTE:** *The corresponding "Bean Counting" worksheet for use in your own district can be found in Part V, Tools of the Trade, Worksheet #5.*

A NOTE ABOUT LABOR TIME: *One of the concerns often expressed in connection with switching from canned beans to dried beans is the need for the staff to sort through the dried beans to check for small rocks and other debris that may have accidentally ended up in the bag during the harvesting process. But the time it takes to sort and clean dried beans won' t likely exceed the time that it takes to open and drain canned beans. Nor will it outweigh the extra cost to dispose of the cans incurred by districts that pay for garbage removal by weight. In the event that switching to dried beans does increase labor time, the lower purchase price of dried beans compared to canned beans can be used to pay for the additional labor hours, thereby helping to improve the economy in your own community.*

HELPFUL TIPS TO SOAKING AND COOKING DRY BEANS

The beauty of beans is that they are so easy to cook. Here are some basic steps for soaking and cooking dried beans:

- *Sort first in a shallow sheet pan. Remove stones.*
- *Rinse beans in a colander to remove dirt.*
- *Soak beans overnight in cold water and refrigerate. This helps the beans to re-hydrate slowly and shortens the cooking time. Lentils do not need to be soaked.*
- *Put beans in a pot with enough fresh cold water to cover them by a few inches.*
- *Discard whatever floats to the top.*
- *Bring to a boil and turn down to a simmer; if heat is too high, beans may toughen. Skim foamy scum from the surface.*
- *Add aromatic vegetables at this point (rather than sooner) so that they don't interfere with skimming the surface of the beans.*
- *Season beans with salt and pepper about 20–30 minutes before they are done.*

QUICK-SOAK METHOD *When time is limited, you can wash and pick over beans and put them into a stockpot with water that covers beans by 3 inches. Bring to a boil. Boil for 10 minutes to remove toxins. Then cover the pot and soak for 1 hour. Discard soaking water, add fresh water, and cook until tender.*

- *As a general rule of thumb, 1 cup of dried beans will yield about 2½–3 cups of cooked beans.*

STRATEGIC USE OF KITCHEN EQUIPMENT *Steam-jacketed kettles, stove-top pressure cookers, and industrial steamers are all examples of equipment ideally suited for cooking large batches of dried beans.*

WORK AHEAD *Cook beans a day or two ahead, cool down in accordance with standard safe food handling protocols, and reheat on the day of service.*

Produce Loot

While an apple a day may not be enough to keep the doctor away, increased consumption of fresh fruits and vegetables is essential to a healthy diet. The good news is that fresh fruits and vegetables are actually quite popular with students at all grade levels.

ATTITUDE IS CONTAGIOUS: *While there will always be children who, through various stages of their development, refuse to eat green food, children's attitudes toward produce are often linked to the messages they receive about it from the adults around them. Rarely is a child who hears an adult say, "You won't like it," going to try it.*

There's a story that goes like this: In America, moms say, "Eat this, it's good for you." In Italy, mammas say, "Eat this, it's good." Always remember that how we speak to children about food is critically important in shaping their overall attitudes toward food.

Salad bars are a popular and effective way to offer students as much fresh produce as possible in the most affordable manner. When used properly, salad bars dramatically improve the quality of the school food, minimize food waste, and significantly reduce expenses and labor hours by eliminating costly portioning containers. From a health perspective, salad bars prove to be a valuable teaching tool by introducing new fruits and vegetables to children and by generating increased interest in eating more fruits and vegetables among students who become empowered to make their own selections.

SAMPLE SALAD BAR LAYOUT

SALAD GREENS Leaf lettuce, romaine, mesclun, spinach or any mix thereof are good options. Iceberg lettuce should be limited, as it is not as nutrient-dense as other options.

FRESH VEGETABLES Options include broccoli, cauliflower, carrots, tomatoes, bell peppers, cucumbers, celery, fresh green or wax beans, snow peas, sugar snap peas, roasted zucchini or yellow squash, roasted potatoes, hot peppers, mushrooms, jicama, onions, radishes, etc. Cold roasted vegetables may also be used.

FRESH FRUIT Options include apples, oranges, kiwi, bananas, pears, grapes, etc. Before placing fresh fruit on the salad bar, first make sure that it is ripe, and then section it into halves or quarters to help encourage students to take only the portion that they will eat and, with respect to younger children, to help them wrap their small hands and mouths around it.

✔ **NOTE:** *Diagrams of both simple and complex salad bar layouts to consider using in your own district can be found in Part V, Tools of the Trade, Diagrams #1 and #2.*

Wherever possible, salad bars should be located either at the beginning of the service line or at the end, just before the cashier's station. In this way, the salad bar will offer students at least two of the five required components required for a federally reimbursable meal (i.e., meat or meat alternative, grain, fruit, vegetable, and milk under the newly mandated "food-based system"). This practice will end the need for the food service staff to prepare and serve additional fruit and vegetable options on the steam table line, eliminating duplication of offerings (and the related costs), and reducing the amount of production time required to prepare vegetables for both the service line and the salad bar.

This technique is instrumental in improving the quality of vegetables served, as hot vegetables served from steam tables are frequently overcooked and lose most of their color and much of their nutritional value by service time. In addition, most steam table lines can then be handled by fewer food service employees (whose jobs then become simply to plate the protein item – typically the entrée – and, if separate, the grain component) as the students come through the service line during meal periods, leaving the extra food service workers free to refresh the salad bar and begin preparing the entrée for the next day's meal.

✔ **NOTE:** *Flow of service diagrams to consider using in your own district can be found in Part V, Tools of the Trade, Diagrams #3 and #4.*

Salad bars are an ideal way to spend the additional funds identified in other sections of *Lunch Money* to improve the quality of school meals. Nevertheless, it is important to keep the cost of a salad bar program to a minimum. When examining your own district's salad bar program, consider centralizing all produce orders at the district level to ensure that the items offered are varied regularly, that all schools are serving the same items, and that the produce ordered is seasonal and within budget.

LOCAL PRODUCE, LOCAL REGULATIONS: *Many states and counties have specific regulations governing when and how school districts can purchase or glean fresh produce directly from local farms. Consult your local health department for assistance in examining the rules regarding water sources, pesticide use, liability insurance, and Hazard Analysis Critical Control Point ("HACCP") plan requirements in your county before contracting directly with any farm.*

BEST PRACTICES FOR SALAD BARS

Salad bars are an amazing way to bring fresh produce to students' lunches. Below are some common best practices for salad bar operations.

TEMPERATURE CONTROL

- *Keep cold foods cold, below 41°F.*
- *Use appropriate cooling systems and containers for your salad bar operation.*
- *Take temperatures of salad bar items and log them appropriately.*
- *If you can, refrigerate containers before filling them.*
- *Cool cooked items properly.*

SAFETY AND EASE-OF-USE

- *Make sure everything is cut to the proper size for the salad bar, especially for younger students.*
- *Prevent cross-contamination during service by filling containers no more than half full.*
- *Have back-up containers available to transfer in.*
- *Do not put old product on top of new, or contaminated product on top of fresh, in the same container.*
- *Have the appropriate utensils in each container.*
- *Have back-up bulk product available to create new containers when necessary.*
- *When breaking down, always discard any product that was out on the salad bar. Items may have been cross-contaminated during service.*

Choice Cuts

When many of us were young, a frequent saying at the dinner table was, "You have two choices: take it or leave it." While that may not have been what we wanted to hear, the experience taught us an important lesson about adapting to circumstances even when we don't get exactly what we want.

Today, school cafeterias all too often resemble a shopping mall food court, with students being offered multiple entrée choices every day. Not only does this encourage a certain sense of entitlement among students, which won't necessarily serve them well in adulthood, but a system that offers many of the same choices every school day paradoxically allows students to choose to eat the same meal every day, thereby limiting the nutritional benefit of a varied diet. Further, when one or more of the choices available are highly processed products, such a system allows 100 percent of the students who make poor eating choices the opportunity to do so 100 percent of the time.

Just as significant in these challenging economic times is the fact that a glut of menu choices typically results in wasted food, wasted time, and wasted money.

One powerful solution to minimizing such waste is the implementation of a cycle menu. A cycle menu is one that repeats frequently throughout the year. The advantages of cycle menus are many, and include: the ability to control inventory and food costs (by purchasing larger quantities less often), the likelihood of food service workers becoming more efficient as they repeat production operations, and the opportunity for children to become more familiar with foods as they see them offered repeatedly throughout the year.

A cycle menu must be sufficiently varied to prevent boredom, both among the food service workers preparing the meals and the students eating them. A good rule of thumb is a four-week cycle for lunch, which will allow menu items to appear approximately once each month. Variations from month-to-month will occur naturally as local, seasonal produce is incorporated as available, but the entrées should remain substantially unchanged.

A four-week cycle menu requires careful planning to ensure, among other things, that multiple high-production days aren't adjacent to each other, that kitchen equipment use is altered from day to day, that a key ingredient doesn't occur in the entrée too frequently during any one week, and that food cost is being kept under control over the course of the entire cycle. Of course, it is essential that the items offered every day of the cycle comprise a reimbursable meal under federal regulations.

Consideration should also be given to providing each day of the week its own "identity," or theme. One possible example might be the following: Mondays are always pasta days, Tuesdays are Mexican food days, Wednesdays are soup and sandwich days, Thursdays are chicken and turkey days, and Fridays are pizza days. (Pizza, when prepared from scratch using wholesome ingredients and served in moderation, can be as healthy as it is popular.) Then, for each of the four days that fall within a category in a given cycle, a different entrée item is served. For example, on Thursdays, the four entrées may be barbecued chicken, roast turkey breast with gravy, herb-roasted chicken, and teriyaki chicken. For both health and financial reasons, emphasis should be placed on varying the protein items during each week to include rice and bean combinations, as well as multiple varieties of meat.

The sample menu below is a good example of what a well-designed cycle menu could look like:

SAMPLE FOUR-WEEK CYCLE LUNCH MENU					
DAY	MONDAY	TUESDAY	WEDNESDAY	THURSDAY	FRIDAY
THEME	Soup & Sandwich	Pasta	Mexican	Poultry	Pizza
WEEK 1	Baked Ham & Cheese Sandwiches (also available without ham)	Spaghetti with or without Meat Sauce	Posolé & Tortillas	Barbecue Chicken & Cornbread	Pizza
WEEK 2	Barbecue Pork Sandwich	Turkey Tetrazzini	Three Bean Chili with Rice	Roast Chicken & Bread Sticks	Pizza
WEEK 3	Hot Chicken Breast Sandwich	Baked Rigatoni	Quesadillas	Roast Turkey with Biscuits & Gravy	Pizza
WEEK 4	Hamburger	Macaroni & Cheese	Bean Burritos	Teriyaki Chicken with Rice	Pizza

— *A variety of fresh fruits and vegetables are offered on our salad bars daily.*

— *Both skim and 1% unflavored milk are offered daily.*

— *All bread products offered, including our pizza, contain at least 50% whole grains.*

✔ **NOTE:** *The corresponding "Cycle Menu Calendar" worksheet for use in your own district can be found in Part V, Tools of the Trade, Worksheet #8.*

When it comes to breakfast, most students and adults alike are in the habit of eating the same or similar foods every day. As a result, a one-week breakfast cycle menu is typically adequate. To help avoid extreme spikes in students' blood sugar levels and to keep students feeling sated until lunchtime, the emphasis in the breakfast cycle menu should be on proteins, whole grains, and fresh fruits. A sample one-week breakfast cycle menu, suitable for Breakfast in the Classroom programs, can be found in Big Breakfast Bucks, below.

THE ADVANTAGES OF CYCLE MENUS WITH ONE ENTRÉE DAILY

CONSISTENCY: *Students, parents and food service staff all know what to expect and when to expect it.*

VARIETY: *A four-week cycle offers 20 different entrée choices over the course of a single month.*

FAMILARITY: *Repeating a cycle menu monthly provides students with the opportunity to get used to the look and taste of menu items.*

EFFICIENCY: *Cycle menus provide food service staff with the opportunity to become proficient at preparing menu items without the boredom inherent in daily repetition, and enable them to work ahead.*

PLANNING: *Food service staff is better able to manage purchasing, inventory control, and production schedules when following a familiar cycle menu.*

ECONOMIES OF MOTION & SCALE: *Serving one daily entrée reduces overall preparation time for food, enabling food service staff to spend more time preparing scratch-cooked meals.*

WASTE REDUCTION: *When multiple entrées are served each day, the tendency of the food service staff is to overproduce each one because there is no way to be sure how many students will choose each entrée. The more choices there are, the more overproduction results. Limiting the entrées to one each day keeps the wasted food to a minimum. And less wasted food equals less wasted money.*

COMMUNITY BUILDING: *Sharing common food gives children a common experience and helps build a sense of community.*

PLANNING FOR VARIETY

While less is more when it comes to entrées, you can still offer students options every day by being creative with your standard menu choices.

OFFER MULTIPLE VERSIONS OF THE SAME ENTRÉE: *Provide two varieties of the same entrée (for example, spaghetti with or without meat sauce, or roast chicken with or without barbecue sauce).*

EXPAND THE SELECTIONS ON THE SALAD BAR: *Provide protein and grain choices (such as cheese and legumes, and grain salad such as couscous, rice, quinoa, and wheat berry salads) on the salad bar, in addition to fresh fruits and vegetables. Doing so will allow students who so choose to eat a complete meal without ordering the entrée.*

USE YOUR COMMON SENSES WHEN PLANNING YOUR MENU: *Eating employs all five senses: sight, hearing, taste, touch, and smell. Build variety into your menu naturally by altering the color, texture, and flavor of the entrées in any given week.*

EMBRACE NOSTALGIA: *Remember the old days when Americans ate a cold sandwich for lunch, made with fresh ingredients? Even in the twenty-first century, there's nothing wrong with that. Offering a tuna, egg, or chicken salad sandwich as an option is a simple, traditional, delicious, and affordable way to feed those students who won' t or can' t eat the entrée of the day.*

À LA CARTE VERSUS REIMBURSABLE MEALS

One of the most controversial topics in school food reform is à la carte sales, sometime referred to as "competitive foods."

Few will deny that items typically sold through à la carte programs and in school vending machines are usually highly processed products filled with salt, sugars, fats, and preservatives. Even so-called "healthier" choices are often riddled with empty calories and chemical additives. Also distressing is the fact that the availability of snack items for sale is stigmatizing for those students who do not have the financial means to purchase them. In effect, offering à la carte products in schools gives rise to de facto categorization of those students who have money to spend and those who do not.

Of course, the argument for allowing à la carte sales in schools is that it often brings additional revenue into districts that are particularly strapped for cash in these tough economic times. The reality, however, is that the net proceeds from à la carte sales (taking into consideration the cost to the school district of the products, the labor spent displaying and inventorying them, loss, theft, etc.) are often far less than imagined.

Another concern often expressed by food service workers in secondary schools is that, without the presence of à la carte options, older students will flee the campus during meal periods.

One way to retain the appearance of à la carte sales, while ensuring that every menu option offered can be part of a reimbursable meal, is to replace the foods available at existing à la carte lines with creative options that, when combined, constitute a reimbursable meal. For example, a homemade smoothie (made with commodity frozen fruit, yogurt, and milk) offered along with a whole grain roll and carrot sticks, can constitute a reimbursable meal that is popular with kids of all ages. In addition, this option would allow those students who are eligible for free or reduced meals to eat the same food as the paying students, would ensure that the students are being fed in a healthful manner, and would help guarantee that the district is maximizing its federal meal reimbursements.

Packaging Pennies

Rare is the person who isn't excited to receive a beautiful package carefully wrapped in the finest paper and adorned with an elaborate bow. Entire stores are dedicated to satisfying such desires by selling gift wrap in every texture, pattern and color, and ribbons of every width, weight and design. Full-color magazines are filled with photographs, diagrams, and advice about the meticulous art of gift-wrapping. Some even encourage the festive wrapping of items not intended to be gifts at all, such as the flower pots next to the sofa, the candy bowls on the buffet, and the picture frames hanging on the wall, all in an effort to maximize the merriment.

Today, elaborate wrapping, once reserved for birthdays and holidays, has seeped into our everyday lives almost without notice and without the splendor celebrated by glossy magazine articles. Moreover, all this wrapping goes well beyond any utilitarian function.

In many school kitchens, food service workers spend hours each day packaging meals – and parts of meals – as if working on an assembly line in Henry Ford's first shop. Sandwiches are wrapped in foil, canned fruit is scooped into plastic cups, cakes squares are placed into styrofoam bowls, and tater tots are nested in paper boats, to cite just a few examples. Often multiple items, having already been packaged once, are then gathered together and assembled for another layer of wrapping in plastic clamshells of varying sizes held closed by a layer or two of clear plastic wrap. And, as a final act of fortification, the pans in which the food is placed for service are lined with giant plastic bags aptly dubbed "pan liners." If Santa employed similar wrapping techniques for his gifts, he would never complete his task in a mere 365 days.

And, he might go bankrupt.

The packaging used in school meal service is costly, both to the environment and to a school food service department's bottom line. And the labor hours spent wrapping items that could be served in simpler ways is a waste of both time and money.

Consider, for example, the practice in many schools, in which the same food service workers who spend hours stuffing plastic cups with celery sticks and paper cups with oranges, then stand behind the service line during meal periods and place the same plastic and paper cups on the students' trays. Might their time – and the money to pay for it – be better spent filling a salad bar with those celery sticks and oranges so that the students can help themselves, leaving the food service workers free to begin prepping the entrée for the next day and replenishing the salad bar?

In reviewing your own district's use of wrapping and packaging supplies, begin by making a list of those you purchase during the year and the total amount of money you spend on them. Your list may include the following items in various sizes:

- ❑ Styrofoam clamshells
- ❑ Plastic clamshells
- ❑ Paper boats
- ❑ Paper sandwich wrappers
- ❑ Wax sandwich wrappers
- ❑ Foil sandwich wrappers
- ❑ Plastic serving cups
- ❑ Lids for plastic serving cups
- ❑ Paper serving cups
- ❑ Paper soufflé cups
- ❑ Plastic parfait cups
- ❑ Lids for plastic parfait cups
- ❑ Plastic beverage cups
- ❑ Paper beverage cups
- ❑ Styrofoam beverage cups
- ❑ Styrofoam trays
- ❑ Styrofoam bowls
- ❑ Styrofoam plates
- ❑ Paper plates
- ❑ Plastic hotel pan liners

Once you have completed your list and added up the costs, you will probably be shocked by the number of digits following the dollar sign. With that inspiration in hand, take the list with you on a tour of your cafeteria. Observe the number of hours that the food service workers spend on the process of packaging. Reflect on the reasons for the current system and begin to strategize alternative solutions. Be sure to ask the food service workers themselves for ideas. Would service be just as easy if sandwiches were placed in a hotel pan with a piece of parchment separating the layers? Would compartmentalized trays allow for service of food items directly on the tray? How much of the wrapping is simply because we think the kids like it better, and is that really an adequate reason to spend money that could instead be used to purchase fresh produce or better quality meat products?

Reducing the amount of disposables used in food service will save money and often save time. Just as important, it will teach students that, counter to popular culture, they do not have to be part of a "throw away society" in which everything comes at a cost but little is valued.

BIG EXPENSES COME IN SMALL PACKAGES

If your district is using those tiny single portion packets of ketchup, mustard, mayonnaise, relish, soy sauce, hot sauce, honey, jam, pancake syrup, and the like, you are probably spending far more money than necessary. On average, those little packets costs from 2 to 9 cents each, and significantly more for such items as cream cheese and salad dressings.

A far more affordable option is to purchase the condiments in one-gallon containers. Most of them can then be poured in squeeze bottles and placed at the end of the service line or on a small table in the cafeteria near the salad bar. For those condiments that are not "squeezable," small bowls with spoons or butter knives usually do the trick. While some effort may be required to fill and clean the bottles and bowls, and to make sure proper temperatures are maintained during service, the work involved is a small price to pay for saving so much.

Fork It Over

A happy time in the life of many parents is the day their baby learns to use a spoon. The event is accompanied by shouts of glee, the flash of cameras, proud phone calls to grandparents, and the inevitable wiping up of the near misses. Indeed, the symbolism of flatware and its use is so significant that the birth of many children is celebrated with the gift of a tiny engraved silver spoon.

By the time those same children arrive at school, however, the importance and value of flatware is often nowhere to be found. Instead, students are greeted with disposable spoons, forks, knives and, more recently, that plasticized hybrid of the late twentieth century, the spork.

A FEW WORDS ABOUT SPORKS: *Financial considerations aside, serious thought should be given to whether sporks are really appropriate for school food service operations. While sporks appear to be the ideal compromise between a spoon and a fork, it is the rare child (or adult, for that matter) who can successfully use a spork to stab a piece of meat or lettuce or to eat soup without spilling. While sporks may have a valid place in some settings, a school — where children are sent to learn — is not one of them. Teaching students the knowledge and skills that will help them thrive in professional settings is one of the ultimate goals of education. Using school meal periods to help students master the skill of properly using forks, spoons, and knives will not only help them enjoy their meals now, it may very well help them during future job interviews and business lunches. We must remember that learning in a school does not stop at the classroom door; the skills students learn in the cafeteria can help them to earn a living to pay for their meals when they reach adulthood.*

But lurking beneath the convenience and modernity of disposable flatware is not only the "picnicization" of every meal, but the negative environmental impact and wasted money – particularly in districts that have functioning mechanical dishwashers in their schools.

EXAMPLE

COST SAVINGS BY REPLACING DISPOSABLE FLATWARE WITH REUSABLE FLATWARE

Meanswell School District serves lunch to an average of 5,000 students and breakfast to an average 1,225 students on each day of the 175-day school year. Every child served gets a disposable plastic fork with each meal. Meanswell pays 2 cents for each fork. The Meanswell Food Service Director makes a call to the district's equipment supplier and learns that reusable metal forks are available for purchase at $1.20 per case of a dozen.

CALCULATING THE COST OF DISPOSABLE FORKS

STEP ONE CALCULATE THE NUMBER OF DISPOSABLE FORKS USED PER SCHOOL YEAR

1.	Number of lunches served per day		5,000
2.	Number of breakfasts served per day	+	1,225
3.	Total number of meals served per day *(Add lines 1 and 2, above)*		6,225
4.	Number of disposable forks used per meal	x	1
5.	Number of disposable forks used per day *(Multiply line 3 by line 4, above)*		6,225
6.	Number of days per school year	x	175
7.	**Number of disposable forks used per School Year** *(Multiply line 5 by line 6, above)*		**1,089,375**

STEP TWO CALCULATE THE COST OF DISPOSABLE FORKS PER SCHOOL YEAR

6.	Number of disposable forks used per school year *(Insert from line 5, above)*		1,089,375
7.	Cost per disposable fork	x	$ .02 ea
8.	**Cost for disposable forks per school year** *(Multiply line 6 by line 7, above)*		**$ 21,787.50**

CALCULATING THE COST OF REUSABLE FORKS

STEP THREE CALCULATE THE NUMBER OF REUSABLE FORKS NEEDED PER SCHOOL YEAR

9.	Total number of meals served per day *(Insert from line 3, above)*		6,225
10.	Number of reusable forks used per meal	x	1
11.	**Total number of reusable forks needed per year** *(Multiply line 9 by line 10, above)*		**6,225**

STEP FOUR CALCULATE THE COST OF REUSABLE FORKS PER SCHOOL YEAR

12.	Cost per case of reusable forks		$ 1.20 cs
13.	Number of reusable forks per case	÷	12
14.	Cost per disposable fork *(Divide line 12 by line 13, above)*		$ .10 ea
15.	Total number of reusable forks needed per year *(Insert from line 11, above)*	x	6,225
16.	**Cost for reusable forks per school year**		**$ 622.50**

CALCULATING THE COST SAVINGS OF SWITCHING TO REUSABLE FORKS

STEP FIVE CALCULATE THE COST SAVINGS PER SCHOOL YEAR OF SWITCHING TO REUSABLE FORKS

17.	Cost for disposable forks per school year *(Insert from line 8, above)*		$ 21,787.50
18.	Cost for reusable forks per school year	–	$ 622.50
19.	**Cost Savings Per School Year of Switching to Reusable Forks** *(Subtract line 18 from line 17, above)*		**$ 21,625.00**

✔ **NOTE:** *The corresponding "Fork It Over" worksheet for use in your own district can be found in Part V, Tools of the Trade, Worksheet #6.*

SOME THINGS TO CONSIDER WHEN SWITCHING TO REUSABLE FLATWARE

- *To help ensure that students don' t accidentally (or accidentally on purpose) throw the reusable flatware in the trash when clearing their trays, leave a bus tub filled with soapy water on a small cart or table next to the trash cans. Make a student feel special by asking him or her to stand next to the bus tub and make sure that the other students use it. Industrial magnets in a range of sizes and prices are available for trash cans to attract stainless flatware that has failed to make it into the bus tubs.*

- *Use some or all of the savings on the purchase price of reusable flatware to increase the hours of part-time employees, thereby moving revenue from the coffers of an unknown manufacturer of disposables into the pockets of a local employee who probably lives in your own community.*

- *Talk to your district's science teachers about turning the introduction of reusable flatware into a lesson about ecology and environmental stewardship.*

Taking Stock

Countless children's books take place behind the creaky doors of dusty attics, where mysteries of the past are unlocked when long-neglected bureaus, trunks and satchels are suddenly rediscovered. While these childhood tales typically end in smiles, the same cannot always be said when long-lost cases of food and supplies are unearthed in schools.

School food service operations are replete with storage locations for food and supplies. District warehouses, walk-in coolers and freezers, reach-in coolers and freezers, dry storage rooms, worktable drawers, and even kitchen offices and hallways, are often filled to capacity with products that were purchased with the cold, hard cash of the food service department's limited budget. Knowing what you have on hand, how much you have on hand, how much you paid for it, and how much longer you can keep it before its useful life expires, are all critical to operating within a budget, regardless of its size.

The technical term for what and how much you have on hand is called "inventory," and the process of taking inventory is often described as mysterious, tedious, confusing, boring, or laborious. However, taking inventory is also an informative process that, in the end, is well worth the time and effort spent to do it accurately.

A school district should think of its inventory as its bank vault. Knowing the value of its contents will help you better manage your budget because whatever cash is tied up in the value of the food and supplies on the shelves is cash that is unavailable for other needs that may be more urgent or more important. A few examples of inventory practices that could be improved are provided below:

- A recipe calls for 32 pounds of raw hamburger meat. A full case contains 40 pounds. The remaining 8 pounds are carefully wrapped and labeled, but are quickly forgotten at the back of the freezer in a corner with other "leftovers."
- A charming salesman convinces a purchasing manager to order a few dozen extra cases of dried oregano, saying, "You never know when there's going to be a crop failure that might drive up the prices."
- One school cafeteria in the district has an overabundance of unused hotel pans in its kitchen, along with a box of brand new knives and scoops in its storeroom. Another school in the same district is in need of additional hotel pans, knives and scoops, so it places an order with the equipment supply company.
- When conducting a thorough cleaning of the kitchen at the end of the school year, the staff discards multiple bags and boxes of food that aren't labeled or that list "use by" dates that have expired.

Each of these examples might rightfully be compared to setting fire to a mattress full of cash, or at least to misplacing the mattress.

To keep waste to a minimum and successfully manage cash flow, the focus should be on keeping inventory as low as possible. This can be accomplished by ordering no more than absolutely necessary, keeping close track of exactly what is on hand, and using it as quickly as possible.

BASIC INVENTORY TERMINOLOGY

There are a few basic concepts about taking inventory that, once understood, help make the process easier and more accurate:

- *The number of "units" of a product refers to the standard way in which you purchase the product. For example, you may order raw chicken in 40-pound cases, so the number of units of raw chicken would mean the number of 40-pound cases that you have on hand. Alternatively, you may order turkey breasts by the piece, so the number of units when inventorying turkey breasts would be the actual number of turkey breasts that you have on hand.*

- *The minimum number of units that you want to have on hand of any particular product is called the "par stock" for that product.*

- *The number of units of a product you have on hand now times the price that you paid for each unit equals the value on hand of that product.*

- *When you add up the value of all of the products you have on hand, the result will be the total value of your inventory on hand.*

- *If you subtract the number of units of a product you currently have on hand from the number of units of the same product you had on hand the last time you took inventory, then add the number of units that were delivered during the same period, the result should be the number of units of that product that you actually used during the inventory period. You should be able to compare the number of units the recipes required during the inventory period to the number of units that you used during that period to help alert you to theft or unnecessary waste.*

- *"FIFO" literally means "first in, first out," and refers to the practice of using up product that was delivered first before using product that was delivered more recently.*

In districts in which schools are all on the same computer network, a networked inventory system can help streamline ordering and include controls to help prevent employees from ordering more than their kitchens need. Whether networked or not, a district's inventory charts, order forms, production records, and even recipes, should all use standardized product names and unit sizes in order to help prevent confusion and mistakes. Consistent use of product categories will also help create a uniform inventory system that is easy to use and more likely to be accurate. Such categories may include:

- Produce
- Meat
- Dairy
- Dry goods
- Paper Products

Some categories can be further subdivided into fresh, frozen, and canned, and their exact location within a kitchen can be identified. While most school food service departments take inventory anywhere from once a month to twice a year, the practice of taking inventory on a weekly or twice-monthly basis will provide the district with a more timely and accurate value of the products it has on hand. It will also help make sure that all of the food and supplies on hand are being used quickly and completely for the benefit of the students in the district, rather than remaining on the shelves like gems in an attic.

SAMPLE INVENTORY ON HAND RECORD

DATE: November 30, 2011

SITE: Dobetter Middle School

STORAGE LOCATION: Walk-In Freezer

ITEM	UNIT OF MEASURE	PAR STOCK	NUMBER OF UNITS ON HAND	X	COST PER UNIT	=	VALUE ON HAND
8-pc Chicken	40# case	2 cs	1/2 cs	X	$100	=	$50
Whole Wheat Bagels	120/case	1 cs	1 cs	X	$96	=	$96
Peas	20# case	6 cs	2 cs	X	$35	=	$70
Blueberries	20# case	3 cs	1 cs	X	$40	=	$40
Hamburger Patties (raw)	40# case	3 cs	1 cs	X	$80	=	$80
BRT Pork Roast (uncooked)	20# each	4 ea	2 ea	X	$50	=	$100
				X		=	
				X		=	
				X		=	
				X		=	
				X		=	
				X		=	

NOTES:

✔ **NOTE:** *The corresponding "Inventory on Hand Record" worksheet for use in your own district can be found in Part V, Tools of the Trade, Worksheet #9.*

SAMPLE INVENTORY USE RECORD

DATE: November 30, 2011

SITE: Dobetter Middle School

STORAGE LOCATION: Walk-In Freezer

ITEM	UNIT OF MEASURE	NUMBER OF UNITS ON HAND AT LAST INVENTORY	+	NUMBER OF UNITS RECEIVED SINCE LAST INVENTORY	–	NUMBER OF UNITS CURRENTLY ON HAND	=	UNITS USED DURING INVENTORY PERIOD
8-pc Chicken	40# case	1 cs	+	2 cs	–	1/2 cs	=	2 1/2 cs
Whole Wheat Bagels	120/ case	2 cs	+	4 cs	–	1 cs	=	5 cs
Peas	20# case	2 cs	+	4 cs	–	2 cs	=	4 cs
Blueberries	20# case	3 cs	+	0 cs	–	1 cs	=	2 cs
Hamburger Patties (raw)	40# case	2 cs	+	1 cs	–	1 cs	=	2 cs
BRT Pork Roast (uncooked)	20# each	4 ea	+	6 ea	–	2 cs	=	8 cs
			+		–		=	
			+		–		=	
			+		–		=	

NOTES:

✔ **NOTE:** *The corresponding "Inventory Use Record" worksheet for use in your own district can be found in Part V, Tools of the Trade, Worksheet #10.*

Waste Not, Want Not

A charming elderly man once told the story of his experience in New Guinea during World War II. He never fired a single shot, nor was he ever caught in the crosshairs of an enemy's weapon. While he was fortunate to have escaped battle during the war, he did not escape hunger; many months passed during which food was scarce. When a supply ship finally arrived and a single canned peach half was rationed out to each soldier, he promptly dropped his on the beach. Whether his clumsiness was a result of faintness or excitement, he couldn't remember. What he did recall was picking up that canned peach and eating it anyway, sand and all. He claimed it was the most delicious bite of food he had ever tasted.

The many prosperous years that so many Americans experienced after World War II seem to have resulted in a certain unconscious disregard for the inherent worth of food. In school cafeterias, this often manifests itself as 40-gallon garbage cans filled with uneaten meals because students weren't given enough time to wait in line, pick up their food, and sit down to eat. In school kitchens, staff members often discard still more food because they haven't been adequately trained in proper product identification, handling, storage, and inventory techniques. It should come as no surprise that wasted food always results in wasted money.

While the ways in which any particular food service operation can avoid waste vary from kitchen to kitchen, awareness and consistent practice of a few guidelines will help keep waste to a minimum (and more money in your budget):

- Get what you pay for. Make sure that your purveyors are delivering what you order and are doing so in an acceptable manner.
- Be able to identify produce, meat, and dairy products that are damaged, tainted, or past their prime so that you don't accidentally accept delivery of items you can't use or mistakenly discard items that are still in perfectly good condition.
- Understand the concept and value of trim loss, i.e., the amount of a product that is removed and not used in the production of a specific recipe. Identify ways in which trim loss can be used for other purposes, for example, stocks, soups, and school garden compost.
- Avoid the temptation to order more product than you need, prepare too much food, and serve portion sizes larger than required.

Beginning to identify and remedy profligate conditions will result in more money for higher quality ingredients, less waste in an atmosphere in which resources are scarce, and greater opportunity to model environmentally and socially responsible behavior to the vigilant students who watch and learn from every example.

GETTING WHAT YOU PAY FOR *Among some vendors, schools are known as an easy place to deliver less-than-perfect goods. The belief that school food service workers are either too busy or too ill-informed to notice being shorted on an order or to recognize inferior goods can be costly to your operation, both in terms of time and money. Help ensure that you are not a victim of this practice by following these guidelines:*

- *Know what you ordered, how much, what size, and whether you are to receive it fresh, frozen, dried, etc.*
- *Know what was delivered, how much was delivered, in what form it was delivered, what condition it was in, and the temperature at which it arrived.*
- *Know whether you received exactly what you ordered from each vendor, and whether everything that arrived was in acceptable condition.*
- *Do not accept delivery of anything that you either did not order or that is not in acceptable condition, unless absolutely necessary. Follow up immediately with your sales representative to ensure that you are given full financial credit for erroneous deliveries and poor quality products.*
- *Respectfully request that deliveries not be made during meal periods when you are too busy to properly check them in. If your request is ignored, politely ask the driver to return at a later time or give him something to eat, ask him to wait in the truck, and tell him you will check the order in as soon as the meal period ends.*

UNDERSTANDING TRIM LOSS

Understanding the concept of "Trim Loss" and its value will encourage you to minimize waste.

"TRIM LOSS" *is the amount of a product that is removed and not used in the production of a specific recipe. For example, when a carrot is peeled before slicing, the peel and the ends are considered the trim and has a dollar value that can be assigned to it.*

Determine the amount of trim loss by weighing the product before doing anything to it (the "as purchased" weight) and weighing it again after you have trimmed and peeled it (the "usable portion"). The difference between the two weights is the amount of trim loss:

As Purchased Weight – Usable Portion Weight = Trim Loss

You can determine the value of your Trim Loss by multiplying the number of pounds of Trim Loss by the price you paid per pound:

Trim Loss in Pounds x Price Paid per Pound = Dollar Value of Trim Loss

EXAMPLE

Imagine that a 50 pound bag of raw carrots costs $62.50, or $1.25 per pound:

$62.50 ÷ 50 lbs = $1.25 per lb

If, after the carrots are peeled, you are left with 45 usable pounds of carrots, the Trim Loss is 5 pounds:

50 lbs – 45 lbs = 5 lbs

At $1.25 per pound, your Trim Loss has a total dollar value of $6.25:

$1.25 per lb x 5 lbs = $6.25 per lb

UNDERSTANDING YIELD PERCENTAGE

Knowing how to use Yield Percentage when calculating your food cost will help you stay on budget.

"YIELD PERCENTAGE" *is the percentage of the original product that you can actually use after you've trimmed and peeled it, and is calculated by dividing the Usable Portion Weight by the As Purchased Weight:*

Usable Portion Weight ÷ As Purchased Weight = Yield Percentage

The yield percentage will help you properly cost recipes. To calculate the cost per usable pound, for example, you would divide the Price Paid per Pound As Purchased by the Yield Percentage:

Price Paid per Pound As Purchased ÷ Yield Percentage = Cost per Usable Pound

EXAMPLE

A roasted carrot recipe requires 8 pounds of peeled carrots. Imagine that a 50 pound bag of carrots costs $62.50, or $1.25 per pound ($62.50 ÷ 50 lbs = $1.25 per lb). After the carrots are peeled, you are left with 45 pounds of usable carrots. To determine the actual cost per pound of the usable portion, we use the following two formulas:

1. ***45 lbs Usable Portion Weight ÷ 50 lbs As Purchased Weight = 90% Yield Percentage***
2. ***$1.25 Price Paid per Pound As Purchased ÷ 90% (or .90) Yield Percentage = $1.39 Cost per Usable Pound***

Finally, when calculating the food cost of a recipe calling for a product that involves Trim Loss (such as carrots, onions, potatoes, celery, lettuce), multiply the number of pounds needed for the recipe by the Cost per Usable Pound, not by the Price per Pound as Purchased:

8 lbs x $1.39 = $11.12 food cost for the carrots used in the recipe

Note that if you had failed to take Trim Loss into consideration and calculated your food cost for the recipe using the Price Paid per Pound as Purchased of $1.25, you would have underestimated the cost by $1.12:

8 lbs x $1.25 = $10.00

Big Breakfast Bucks

Breakfast is often said to be the most important meal of the day, especially for children. Given that eating breakfast has been shown to help decrease behavioral issues and improve attendance, breakfast habits of schoolchildren are of paramount importance.[16]

The benefits of eating before undertaking difficult intellectual challenges hasn't escaped the notice of many educators, who often request that breakfast be served in their classrooms on state aptitude testing days. Nonetheless, many principals, teachers, and custodians, reluctant to break out of old patterns, hesitate to introduce Breakfast in the Classroom ("BIC") programs – in which every child is served breakfast every day – into their schools.

Logic dictates, however, that if students score higher when they are fed properly before taking a test, they will test higher still if fed when they are *learning* the materials that will later be covered on the test. Moreover, BIC programs ensure that all students start their academic day on a level playing field, giving them the nourishment they need to learn[17] and to do well in math, science, and on standardized exams.[18]

In addition, BIC programs decrease the stress level of students who are running late and may not have had time to eat either at home or at school, and eliminate the stigma that many students who are eligible for free or reduced meals feel when eating school breakfast in the cafeteria. They also diminish the suspicion among some parents that their children are not really being fed at school. In sum, BIC programs ensure that every student in every classroom begins each school day with the same opportunity for success.

Perhaps of equal importance in today's economy is the potential for significant enhancement to the district's revenue that can be generated by BIC programs in schools in which "at least 40 percent of the lunches served to students at the school in the second preceding school year were served free or at a reduced price," otherwise known as "Severe Need" schools.[19] In other words, if at least four out of every ten lunches served in a school two school years earlier were served to students who were eligible for either free or reduced meals, the school is classified as Severe Need.

Because federal funding for the School Breakfast Program in Severe Needs schools is considerably higher than the funding in more affluent schools, and due to the relatively low cost of food served at breakfast (when compared to lunch), a BIC program can give a meaningful financial boost to such schools.

By way of explanation, when analyzing the cost of a meal, three factors must be considered: (1) fixed costs (such as rent and utilities), (2) labor costs, and (3) food cost. In the case of most food service operations, fixed costs generally remain relatively constant regardless of the number of meals being served. So, for purposes of calculating the financial impact of implementing a BIC program,

MEAL, SNACK AND MILK PAYMENTS TO STATES AND SCHOOL FOOD AUTHORITIES *Expressed in Dollars or Fractions Thereof. Effective from July 1, 2011 —June 30, 2012*			
SCHOOL BREAKFAST PROGRAM		**NON-SEVERE NEED**	**SEVERE NEED**
Contiguous States	Paid	.27	.27
	Reduced Price	1.21	1.50
	Free	1.51	1.80
Alaska	Paid	.40	.40
	Reduced Price	2.11	2.58
	Free	2.41	2.88
Hawaii	Paid	.30	.30
	Reduced Price	1.46	1.80
	Free	1.76	2.10

fixed costs become largely irrelevant. With respect to labor costs, school districts that are already employing staff to set up, serve, and break down breakfast in the cafeteria on a daily basis are usually already adequately staffed to handle the production required for BIC programs. Therefore, the only significant cost per meal that must be offset against revenue generated is the food cost.

Food cost for school breakfast typically ranges from 65 to 80 cents per meal. As a result, the federal (and state) reimbursement revenue generated by serving breakfast to all students every day in the classroom through BIC programs can significantly exceed the food costs incurred and, consequently, result in a considerable net financial gain for the district.

EXAMPLE

CALCULATING COSTS FOR BREAKFAST IN THE CLASSROOM

There are 5,000 students in the Meanswell School District. Of the 5,000 students, 3,000 are eligible for free meals, 500 are eligible for reduced meals, and 1,500 are not eligible for either free or reduced meals. Meanswell currently offers breakfast in the cafeterias before school every morning during the 175-day school year, but the average daily participation is low: 1,000 students eligible for free meals, 125 eligible for reduced meals, and 100 eligible for neither free nor reduced meals. Meanswell charges the following prices for breakfast: 30 cents for students eligible for reduced meals, and $1.50 for students who are not eligible for either free or reduced meals. What would be the potential increase in net revenue to Meanswell if it shifts from serving breakfast in the cafeteria to serving breakfast in the classroom?

DETERMINE YOUR CONSTANTS FOR THE YEAR

STEP ONE DETERMINE STUDENT ELIGIBILITY

1.	Total number of students eligible for free meals	3,000
2.	Total number of students eligible for reduced meals	500
3.	Total number of students not eligible for either free or reduced-price meals	1,500
4.	**Total Number of Students** *(Add lines 1, 2 and 3, above)*	**5,000**

STEP TWO DETERMINE CURRENT AVERAGE DAILY PARTICIPATION

5.	Average daily number of students eligible for free meals who eat breakfast	1,000
6.	Average daily number of students eligible for reduced meals who eat breakfast	125
7.	Average daily number of students not eligible for either free or reduced-price meals who eat breakfast	100
8.	**Total Number of Students Currently Participating in Breakfast Program** *(Add lines 5, 6, and 7, above)*	**1,225**

STEP THREE DETERMINE YOUR SALES PRICES

9.	Price paid for breakfast by students eligible for free meals	$	0.00
10.	Price paid for breakfast by students eligible for reduced-price meals	$	.30
11.	Price paid for breakfast by students not eligible for either free or reduced-price meals	$	1.50

STEP FOUR DETERMINE REIMBURSEMENT RATES

12. **Free**

(a)	Federal reimbursement rate for students eligible for free breakfast *(For districts that served 40% or more free or reduced-price lunches during the 2009-2010 school year, insert $1.80; all others insert $1.51.)*	$	1.80
(b)	State reimbursement rate for students eligible for free breakfast	$	0.00
(c)	Other reimbursements for students eligible for free breakfast *(Note: Do not include cash sales on this line.)*	$	0.00
(d)	**Total Reimbursements for Students Eligible for Free Breakfast** *(Add lines 12(a), 12(b) and 12(c), above)*	**$**	**1.80**

13. **Reduced**

(a) Federal reimbursement rate for students eligible for reduced-price breakfast — $ 1.50
(For districts that served 40% or more free or reduced-price lunches during 2009-2010 school year, insert $1.50; all others insert $1.21.)

(b) State reimbursement rate for students eligible for reduced-price breakfast — $ 0.00

(c) Other reimbursements for students eligible for reduced-price breakfast — $ 0.00
(Note: Do not include cash sales on this line.)

(d) Total Reimbursements for Students Eligible for Reduced-Price Breakfast — **$ 1.50**
(Add lines 13(a), 13(b) and 13(c), above)

14. **Paid**

(a) Federal reimbursement rate for students not eligible for either free or reduced-price breakfast — $ .27
(All districts insert $ .27.)

(b) State reimbursement rate for students not eligible for either free or reduced-price breakfast — $ 0.00

(c) Other reimbursement rate for students not eligible for either free or reduced-price breakfast — $ 0.00
(Note: Do not include cash sales on this line.)

(d) Total Reimbursements for Students Not Eligible for Either Free or Reduced-Price Breakfast — **$ .27**
(Add lines 14(a), 14(b) and 14(c), above)

STEP FIVE DETERMINE FOOD COST PER MEAL

15. Average Daily Food Cost per Meal for Breakfast $ .80

STEP SIX
DETERMINE NUMBER OF DAYS PER SCHOOL YEAR

16. Number of Days per School Year on which Breakfast is Served 175

CALCULATE POTENTIAL NET REVENUE FROM BREAKFAST IN THE CLASSROOM

STEP SEVEN CALCULATE POTENTIAL REIMBURSEMENTS PER DAY

17. Total potential reimbursements for students eligible for free breakfast $ 5,400.00
(Multiply line 1 (3,000) by line 12(d) ($ 1.80), above)

18. Total potential reimbursements for students eligible for reduced-price breakfast $ 750.00
(Multiply line 2 (500) by line 13(d) ($ 1.50), above)

19. Total potential reimbursements for students not eligible for either free or reduced-price breakfast $ 405.00
(Multiply line 3 (1,500) by line 14(d) ($ .27), above)

20. **Total Potential Reimbursements per Day** **$ 6,555.00**
(Add lines 17, 18 and 19, above)

STEP EIGHT CALCULATE POTENTIAL TOTAL FOOD COST PER DAY FOR BREAKFAST

21. **Total Potential Food Cost Per Day for Breakfast** **$ 4,000.00**
(Multiply line 4 (5,000) by line 15 ($ .80), above)

STEP NINE CALCULATE POTENTIAL NET REVENUE FROM BREAKFAST IN THE CLASSROOM PER DAY

22. Total Potential Daily Net Revenue from Breakfast in the Classroom **$ 2,555.00**
(Subtract line 21 from line 20, above)

STEP TEN CALCULATE POTENTIAL NET REVENUE FROM BREAKFAST IN THE CLASSROOM PER SCHOOL YEAR

23. Number of school days per year on which breakfast is served x 175
(Insert from line 16, above)

24. Total Potential Annual Net Revenue from Breakfast in the Classroom **$ 447,125.00**
(Multiply line 22 ($ 2,555.00) by line 23 (175), above)

CALCULATE NET REVENUE FOR CURRENT BREAKFAST PROGRAM

STEP ELEVEN CALCULATE CURRENT REIMBURSEMENTS FROM BREAKFAST IN THE CAFETERIA PER DAY

25. Total current reimbursements for students eligible for free breakfast $ 1,800.00
(Multiply line 5 (1,000) by line 12(d) ($ 1.80), above)

26. Total current reimbursements for students eligible for reduced-price breakfast $ 187.50
(Multiply line 6 (125) by line 13(d) ($ 1.50), above)

27. Total current reimbursements for students not eligible for either free or reduced-price breakfast $ 27.00
(Multiply line 7 (100) by line 14(d) ($ .27), above)

28. Total Current Reimbursements from Breakfast per Day **$ 2,014.50**
(Add lines 25, 26 and 27, above)

STEP TWELVE CALCULATE CURRENT REVENUE FROM SALES OF BREAKFAST PER DAY

29. Total current daily revenue from sales of breakfast to students eligible for free breakfast — $ 0.00
(Multiply line 5 (1,000) by line 9 ($ 0.00), above)

30. Total current daily revenue from sales of breakfast to students eligible for reduced-price breakfast — $ 37.50
(Multiply line 6 (125) by line 10 ($ .30), above)

31. Total current daily revenue from sales of breakfast to students not eligible for either free or reduced-price breakfast — $ 150.00
(Multiply line 7 (100) by line 11 ($ 1.50), above)

32. **Total Current Revenues from Sales of Breakfast per day** — **$ 187.50**
(Add lines 29, 30 and 31, above)

STEP THIRTEEN CALCULATE TOTAL CURRENT REVENUE FROM BREAKFAST SALES AND REIMBURSEMENTS PER DAY

33. Total current reimbursements from breakfast per day — $ 2,014.50
(Insert from line 28, above)

34. Total current revenues from sales of breakfast per day — $ 187.50
(Insert from line 32, above)

35. **Total Current Revenue from Breakfast Sales and Reimbursements per Day** — **$ 2,220.00**
(Add lines 33 and 34, above)

STEP FOURTEEN CALCULATE TOTAL CURRENT FOOD COST FOR BREAKFAST PER DAY

36. **Total Current Food Cost for Breakfast per Day** — – **$ 980.00**
(Multiply line 8 (1,225) by line 15 ($ .80), above)

STEP FIFTEEN CALCULATE CURRENT NET REVENUE FROM BREAKFAST PER DAY

37. **Current Net Revenue from Breakfast per Day** $ 1,240.00
(Subtract line 36 from line 35, above)

STEP SIXTEEN CALCULATE CURRENT NET REVENUE FROM BREAKFAST PER SCHOOL YEAR

38. Number of school days per year on which breakfast is served x 175
(Insert from line 16, above)

39. **Total Current Annual Net Revenue from breakfast in the cafeteria** $ 217,000.00
(Multiply line 37 ($ 1,240.00) by line 38 (175), above)

COMPARE POTENTIAL NET REVENUE FOR BIC PROGRAM TO REVENUE FOR CURRENT BREAKFAST PROGRAM

STEP SEVENTEEN CALCULATE POTENTIAL ADDITIONAL NET REVENUE FROM BREAKFAST IN THE CLASSROOM PER SCHOOL YEAR

40. Total potential annual net revenue from breakfast in the classroom $ 447,125.00
(Insert from line 24, above)

41. Total current annual net revenue from breakfast in the cafeteria – $ 217,000.00
(Insert from line 39, above)

42. **Potential Additional Net Revenue per School Year from Switching to a Breakfast in the Classroom Program** $ 230,125.00
(Subtract line 41 from line 40, above)

✔ **NOTE:** *The corresponding "Big Breakfast Bucks" worksheet for use in your own district can be found in Part V, Tools of the Trade, Worksheet #7.*

A NOTE ABOUT LABOR TIME: *As mentioned earlier, it is important to note that labor and overhead expenses rarely increase with the introduction of a Breakfast in the Classroom program in a school that is already offering breakfast in the cafeteria. Where Breakfast in the Classroom is being added to a school in which breakfast was not previously offered at all, additional labor costs may result. In those cases, the total additional labor cost for the year should be subtracted from line 42 for an accurate calculation of Potential Additional Net Revenue from Breakfast in the Classroom.*

UNIVERSAL BREAKFAST IS NOT ALWAYS UNIVERSAL: *Don't mistake a district's "universal breakfast" program for a BIC program; the two are not necessarily the same. Universal breakfast simply means that every child eats breakfast for free; it does not mean that breakfast is being served in the classroom. Many school districts offer free breakfast to all students in the cafeteria each morning but still suffer low participation rates. Consequently, they are missing the opportunity to maximize the revenue-generating potential of a BIC program and to ensure that every child eats breakfast before setting to work at the challenging job of learning. Offering free breakfast every morning to every student in the classroom is the only way to truly make the breakfast meal universal.*

CONSIDERING FOOD QUALITY AND COST FOR A BREAKFAST IN THE CLASSROOM PROGRAM

Of course there's no sense in introducing a BIC program if it simply becomes another opportunity for students to consume more salt, fat, sugars, and artificial colors. Maximize the benefits of your BIC program by ensuring that students are fed in the most healthful manner possible.

Below is a sample breakfast menu that easily lends itself to BIC programs, meets federal guidelines for the food-based system, and — in most regions — will come within the average budget of 80 cents per serving over the course of the week.

SAMPLE FOOD-BASED ONE-WEEK CYCLE BREAKFAST MENU

MONDAY	TUESDAY	WEDNESDAY	THURSDAY	FRIDAY
Hardboiled Egg	Whole Grain Muffin	Yogurt	Whole Grain, Low Sugar Cereal	String Cheese
100% Juice	Orange	Apple	Banana	100% Juice
Whole Grain Bagel	Milk	Whole Grain Roll	Milk	Quick Bread
Milk		Milk		Milk

NOTE: *Be sure to check the current USDA regulations to ensure compliance with portion sizes and calorie limits for relevant grade levels.*

Time Is Money

A memorable line in a song of otherwise questionable humor goes, "If it wasn't for the Lunch Lady, the kids wouldn't eat ya. You should be shakin' her hand and sayin', 'Pleased to meet ya.'"

Sadly, school food service workers rarely receive the appreciation they deserve for their tireless efforts in a job that many people would be unwilling to do themselves. Instead, they serve as the brunt of tasteless jokes, are portrayed as unsightly action figures, are lampooned in comedy skits of dubious wit, and, in recent years, are blamed for childhood obesity in America. As a result, it comes as no surprise that food service workers often feel as if they are the least important staff members in a school district's hierarchy, despite the critically important role they play in students' lives.

When the people who are responsible for feeding our children feel blamed rather than empowered, the path to school food reform can be a long one. The national obesity crisis and the poor quality of the average school meal are merely symptoms of America's broken food system, the myriad causes of which include campaign finance laws, farm subsidies favoring corporate agriculture, and ubiquitous marketing campaigns targeting children. Simply blaming food service workers for those greater social maladies will not improve the quality of school food or the health of our children.

However, treating food service workers as a valuable resource can begin to transform school food from a problem into a solution. By professionalizing food service workers and giving them the skills to maximize productivity, minimize waste, and increase participation, they in turn will help improve their food service department's bottom line.

Some effective approaches for professionalizing school food service workers are:

- Requiring professional attire
- Offering hands-on culinary education
- Providing proper tools and equipment
- Creating strategic work schedules
- Treating school food with respect

DRESS FOR SUCCESS

Dressing school food service workers in professional chef attire is remarkably effective in improving the image of a school food program. White chef jackets and black pants give food service workers a sense of pride and self-respect that may otherwise be lacking, serve as a constant reminder to other school staff members that food service workers have an important job that they take very seriously, and instill students with a sense of trust in the food service workers who they come to view – rightfully so – as professional cooks. In addition, chef uniforms are designed to protect cooks from injuries due to hot pans, splatters, and spills, thereby helping to minimize costly workers' compensation claims. Thus, mandating chef uniforms should be considered essential to safe work practices.

TEACH A MAN TO FISH

An essential step towards professionalizing the school food environment and workforce is providing culinary training for food service workers that builds their skills, awareness, motivation, and self-respect. When executed properly, culinary training transforms food service workers into culinary ambassadors who lead the school food reform movement in their district and embrace their essential role in teaching children about the pleasures and benefits of eating real food prepared in a healthful manner. Moreover, such training creates food service workers who have the knowledge and skills to perform their jobs in the most efficient and cost-effective manner possible.

Many food service workers attend annual classes offered by professional associations and state agencies in which they are taught regulatory compliance and paperwork completion. While these classes are important, professional training for food service workers can't stop there. Cooking is a hands-on job, and the skills required for scratch-cooking can't truly be taught – or learned – through lecture alone. Hands-on kitchen training by practiced chefs who possess extensive experience in both teaching and institutional cooking – as well as healthy doses of humility and patience – will help ensure that food service workers are properly and effectively trained to safely prepare delicious scratch-cooked meals, to skillfully use their kitchen equipment to help manage their time efficiently, to control their inventory and waste in a cost effective manner, and to teach students the joys and benefits of eating real food.

FOR WANT OF A PROPER TOOL

For most districts, building central kitchens and developing district-wide distribution systems may not be financially possible until the money saving and generating techniques in *Lunch Money* have been in place for a few years. But that's no reason to delay consideration of obtaining smaller, more affordable pieces of cooking equipment that can markedly increase the efficiency of the food service workers and the quality of the meals they prepare.

Included on the list of most beneficial and affordable kitchen tools are:

- 8″ chef knives and honing steels
- Ice wands (for rapidly cooling stocks and sauces)
- Immersion blenders (for quickly blending large quantities of sauces, dressings, and smoothies without the time-consuming need to transfer liquids from one container to another)
- Food processors (for chopping, slicing, shredding, and otherwise fabricating large volumes of fresh produce at blazing speeds)
- Sectionizers (for manually slicing oranges, potatoes, and other produce into 8 equal slices)

Before placing an order for new equipment, verify with your equipment purveyor that he or she will contact the manufacturer to schedule proper training for your staff in how to assemble, use, maintain, store, and clean it. A good purveyor will work hard to ensure that you are happy with your purchase.

A TIME FOR EVERY PURPOSE

Though school food service workers have traditionally started their work days early in the morning and finished early in the afternoon, this schedule is not necessarily the best suited for every school food service operation. In some districts, dividing the labor force into two shifts may work more efficiently, particularly in districts with central production kitchens or in schools with small kitchens in which food service workers are currently tripping over each other or waiting for equipment already in use by others. In such cases, the first shift would work traditional hours, starting early and ending shortly after lunch service. The second shift would begin its day shortly before lunch (so that they would be available to assist during meal service) and complete the workday by prepping for the next day, either in the same school or in the central production kitchen. Even a third shift, either to meet additional cooking needs or for cleaning and maintenance, may make sense in some districts.

In addition, some districts may find it beneficial to shift some labor hours from the school year to the summer months even when classes are not in session. This allows districts to take advantage of the wide availability of fresh, local produce at the most affordable prices and to use the savings to employ some of its labor force to "put food by" during harvest season. This scheduling strategy can be an effective method of maximizing labor time, lowering food cost, and increasing the quality of the food served to students during the school year. Historically, "putting food by," which is to say storing food in abundant summer months for consumption during the lean winter months, has meant canning, preserving, and root cellaring. In a contemporary school environment, traditional canning procedures at such high volumes can carry risks of foodborne illness that are not worth taking. Thus, the modern process more typically involves washing and trimming the summer produce and freezing it for use during the school year. Also, depending on available freezer space, some products, such as tomato sauce or squash puree, can be cooked during the summer and frozen for use throughout the year.

LEAD BY EXAMPLE

In far too many school districts, meal periods are such noisy, rushed, chaotic affairs that the school administrators appear to have forgotten that children don't stop learning just because they're in the cafeteria. Embracing school food as a fundamental and critical component of the educational process by supporting food service workers in their efforts to return to scratch-cooked meal preparation will help teach students a skill that will serve them well throughout their lives: the proper way to feed themselves in a healthful and delicious manner.

THE MYTH OF MEALS PER LABOR HOUR

In school food service operations, "Meals per Labor Hour" are the result of dividing the total meals produced and served during a given time period by the total number of labor hours worked during that same time period to produce and serve those meals.

Thus, if three food service workers collectively work a total of 18 hours per day to prepare 360 meals per day, their meals per labor hour equal 20 per day:

Total Meals Produced	*360*
÷ Total Hours Worked	*÷ 18*
Meals per Labor Hour	***20***

That workers should produce a specific number of meals for each hour worked is a commonly-held belief that is often based on misinformation. The reality is that no such "correct" number of meals per labor hour exists, and thus efforts by management to mandate such a number, and attempts by labor to bargain for additional employees as a result of such a number, are equally ill-advised.

For instance, if the three food service workers in the example above have only one oven in their kitchen, they will require more time to produce those 360 meals than if they have four ovens. Similarly, if they are producing 120 servings each of three different entrées, they will likely require more time than if they are producing 360 servings of a single entrée.

A few of the relevant variables that may affect meals per labor hour are:

- *Kitchen design and equipment*
- *Staff training and attire*
- *The length and number of lunch periods*
- *Whether or not disposables are being used for service*
- *Number of items offered on the menu*

Because of the variables from kitchen to kitchen in a school district, the best — and arguably only — use for Meals per Labor Hour calculations is to track the production levels in a kitchen when a staff member or piece of equipment is replaced. If the Meals per Labor Hour decrease immediately thereafter, that can be a valuable clue about the need for additional staff training. Likewise, if Meals per Labor Hour immediately increase, it may be worth investing in that new piece of equipment for other district kitchens or asking the new employee to share his or her time management skills with other staff members.

Show Me The Money

PART IV

Show Me The Money

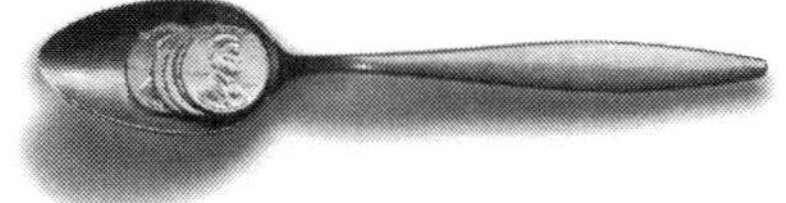

"Starting from scratch is easy;
starting without it is tough."
– *Peter's Almanac*

A SIMULATED SCHOOL FOOD TREASURE HUNT

YOU: A concerned citizen who has just read *Lunch Money: Serving Healthy School Food in a Sick Economy*.

THE SCENE: Dobetter Middle School in Meanswell School District is a large middle school that serves 600 6th through 8th graders. In a happier time, the town of Meanswell was a thriving railroad town in which most of the residents either worked for the railroad or ran their family farms. Today, with rail traffic slowed and farmers struggling to stay afloat, 300 of Dobetter's students are eligible for free meals and 100 are eligible for reduced meals.

YOUR ASSIGNMENT: Visit Dobetter Middle School in Meanswell School District and observe the meals being served and the food service employees at work so that you can help advise them how to make cost-effective improvements to their operation to promote the health and well-being of their students. Use the information, skills, and tools that you've learned in *Lunch Money* to identify ways in which the Meanswell Food Service Department can reduce expenses and increase revenue.

YOUR OBSERVATIONS:

Breakfast

When you walk into the school kitchen at 6:00 AM, you observe the following:

There are three food service workers on staff at Dobetter: Edna, Marcos, and Sue. All of them are already at work. They are surprised to see you because, they say, they rarely get visitors. They tell you to feel free to look around, but that they hope you understand that they have to focus on their work.

For the first 90 minutes of your visit, you observe Edna and Marcos stacking the display racks and counters with individual boxes of cereal, various types of packaged breakfast bars, cartons of orange juice, and plastic bottles of chocolate milk. When they finish, they begin filling what appears to be the salad bar with containers of plastic flatware, napkins, and individual packages of ketchup, hot sauce, assorted jellies, and artificial pancake syrup. Sue spends her time filling sheet pans with frozen potato triangles, frozen pancakes, frozen omelets, and frozen sausage patties, and moving them from the counter to the oven to the hotbox and, finally, to the steam table on the service line. Just before service, Marcos takes the temperatures of all of the hot and cold items being served, and records them in the HACCP log.

When the cafeteria doors open for breakfast at 7:30 AM, about 100 bleary-eyed kids trickle through the line. Edna tends the cash register while Marcos and Sue dish out food and replenish supplies. About 100 more kids slump down at the cafeteria tables but don't go through the service line; some are doing homework, some appear to be napping, and others are busily chatting with friends. A couple hundred more kids are just outside the cafeteria doors hanging out in the hallways.

When the bell rings at 8:05 AM, the cafeteria clears out, and Edna records her morning transactions: today they served breakfast to 80 kids who were eligible for a free breakfast, to 15 kids who paid the reduced price of 30 cents for their breakfast, and to 5 kids who paid $1.50 each for their breakfast. Meanwhile, Marcos gets to work clearing the steamtable, wrapping leftovers, and reshelving unused condiment packages, cereal boxes, and breakfast bars. Sue wipes down the cafeteria tables and chairs, sweeps the kitchen floor, and washes the baking and serving pans used that morning. They finish cleaning up breakfast at 8:30 and begin working on lunch preparation.

Lunch Preparation

Edna focuses her attention on preparing the Three Bean Chili. She proudly tells you that she "makes it from scratch." She cheerfully invites you to follow her to the storeroom and the walk-in freezer while she gathers her ingredients. On her way, she grabs a stainless steel kitchen cart with one wheel that doesn't seem to be working properly. She apologizes and tells you that the task might take longer than it should because she hasn't been able to get anyone to respond to her repeated requests to fix the cart. Once in the storeroom, Edna grabs fresh onions, canned kidney beans, canned pinto beans, canned navy beans, canned tomatoes, and chili powder. She piles them on the broken cart and half pushes, half shoves it back to her work station where she stacks everything on the counter. Then she takes the wobbly cart to the walk-in freezer to get the pre-cooked frozen "beef crumbles." When she opens the freezer door, you are met with a solid wall of cardboard boxes filled with pre-made products. When you ask her what's in all of the boxes, she replies, "Just a bunch of different food things. I'm not exactly sure what it all is. We don't take inventory again until the end of the year. But I know the beef crumbles are in here somewhere."

When she finally moves a couple dozen heavy boxes out of the freezer, she locates the case of beef crumbles and puts it on her cart. As she returns the other boxes to the freezer, she tells you that she had her free commodity beef sent to a processor to turn it into the crumbles because it was cheaper than buying the crumbles from her regular supplier. She estimates that she saves thousands of dollars every year by having her free commodity meat and cheese processed into beef crumbles, pork dippers, hot dogs, corndogs, pre-cooked burgers, chicken patties, chicken nuggets, beef burritos, and pizzas.

Once Edna returns to her work station with the beef crumbles, she begins opening the #10 cans of kidney, pinto, and navy beans, and draining them in large perforated pans. She mentions that this is one of her least favorite parts of her job because the can opener isn't as sharp as it used to be, the empty cans take up so much space in her garbage, and she sometimes cuts herself on the jagged edge of the lids. While the beans are draining, she grabs a paring knife and begins peeling and slicing the onions. Again she apologizes, telling you that her knives are dull so she can't work as quickly as she used to. When she finally finishes chopping the onions, she adds them to the giant steam kettle with the tomatoes, beans, beef crumbles, and chili powder, and starts to crush the empty cans, break down the empty boxes, and clean up her station. You ask her how many servings she is making. She breaks into a smile as she tells you that she's making 200 servings, though she could probably sell 600 servings because her chili is a favorite with the kids.

MENU

Today's Special

Three Bean Chili, Cinnamon Rolls, Tater Tots, Fresh Canned Fruit Cocktail Cups, Cookies, Chocolate Milk

Served Daily!

Pizza, Hot Dogs, Cheeseburgers, Nachos, Chicken Nuggets, Spicy Chicken Patties, Corn Dogs & French Fries

When Marcos finishes getting all of the boxes out of the freezer, he carries them one at a time to his work station. You ask him why he doesn't save himself some time by using a cart, to which he replies that there is only one cart and Edna is using it.

You help Marcos carry boxes over to his station, and he begins to open them and lay their contents out on dozens of sheet pans, which he then loads onto movable racks. He loads up the double-stacked convection oven with as many trays as will fit before returning to his task of filling more sheet pans with more items. You notice that there are two conventional ovens located under the range. You ask Marcos why he isn't using those ovens. He responds, "Because we never use those. I don't even know if they work."

As Marcos works, he tells you that he needs to pan up 150 servings of pizza, 75 hot dogs, 75 corn dogs, 100 cheeseburgers, 100 chicken patties, and enough chicken nuggets for 100 servings. He tells you he's grateful to have Sue there to help him make 100 servings of nachos, pan up all the french fries, tater tots, and cinnamon rolls, portion the fruit cocktail, bake off the cookies, and refill the cooler with plastic bottles of chocolate milk. When someone is out sick, he says, it's a real circus trying to get everything done before the first lunch bell rings.

While listening to Marcos, you do some quick calculations in your head and ask him why he is preparing so many entrées when Edna is already making 200 servings of her famous chili. Marcos doesn't hesitate a moment when he replies, "We never know what the kids are going to order, so we have to make plenty of everything."

You stroll over to Sue's work station, where she meets you with a tired and somewhat sad expression. You ask, "Are you okay?" She tells you that she's thankful to have a job and that she loves the kids, but that she finds her job boring. She says, "I wish we could cook here the way we cook at home. It tastes so much better at home." You ask her if she has ever suggested it to anyone, and she replies, "Nobody listens to us. They don't really even notice us unless something goes wrong."

You give Sue a sympathetic hug and ask her how you can help her with her task at hand. She tells you that she needs to fill 400 plastic cups with 4 ounces of fruit cocktail. She asks you to open the cans while she gathers the cups and puts them on sheet pans. You open #10 can after #10 can of fruit cocktail and drain them in large perforated pans. As soon as Sue finishes loading up the sheet pans with the plastic cups, you both begin using 4-ounce ice cream scoops to portion the product into individual portion cups. Sue seems happy to have the company and tells you that having your help will save her at least an hour.

When you and Sue finish with the fruit cocktail, Sue begins filling sheet pans with french fries and tater tots as you observe and write down a few notes. You notice that Marcos is now putting the heated chicken patties on buns and wrapping each one individually in foil-lined paper. Edna is on the phone placing an order for next week.

You walk over to Marcos and ask him why he's wrapping all of the chicken sandwiches, rather than just keeping them on a covered tray until service. He answers, "Because the kids like them that way. It reminds them of the food court at the mall." Then he asks you if you would mind putting the hot dogs in buns and placing each one in a paper boat so that Sue can put them in the hot box near the service line next to the french fries and tater tots.

As you put on another new pair of plastic gloves so that you can "bun and boat" the hot dogs, you notice that Edna has returned to the kitchen to begin panning up frozen cookie pucks to be baked off just before lunch service begins. She sees you watching her, and she shouts out that the cookies are so much fresher now that they pay one of the students to come in during the period right before lunch and put the warm cookies in small paper bags for service. She flashes you a big smile and says, "Wait 'til you see how cute those little red and white striped bags are! They remind me of popcorn boxes at the movies!"

You see that Sue has now taken the frozen cinnamon rolls out of the oven and is drizzling white frosting from a plastic container onto them. Edna reminds her that, as soon as she's finished with the cinnamon rolls, she needs to line the steam table pans with large plastic bags and then fill the pans with the chili. You're standing fairly close to Sue, so you ask her why the pans need to be lined with plastic bags; she tells you that they're easier to clean that way.

At 11:00 AM, everyone stops working to take their lunch break. Edna and Sue each get a bowl of chili and a cookie, and Marcos gets a plastic clamshell container filled with nachos, and they all walk over to the à la carte display and grab a 24-ounce energy drink and a bag of crunchy cheese chips. Then they sit down at one of the tables and eat quickly while wondering aloud whether there are going to be more staff cuts because of the district's budget crisis. At 11:20 AM, they make their way back into the kitchen to finish setting up before the first lunch bell rings at 11:30 AM.

Lunch Service

When the first group of kids shoves through the cafeteria doors, Edna is back at her cash register, and Marcos and Sue are manning the service line. Marcos fills bowls with chili while Sue hands students plastic clamshells filled with nachos and chicken nuggets, and paper boats filled with sandwiches, corn dogs, and pizza. She asks each one if they would rather have tater tots or french fries. Nearly every kid grabs a bag of cookies and a carton of chocolate milk. You watch more kids stop at the à la carte coolers and racks to add chips or sports drinks to their tray; you're pretty sure you spotted at least two kids sneak the snacks under their jackets before checking out with Edna.

After checking out, the kids proceed to the "salad bar" to load up on condiment packages for their sandwiches, and sit down to eat. Having a good sense of how the rest of the lunch period will go, you wave your goodbyes to Edna, Marcos, and Sue, and thank them for welcoming you into their world.

YOUR RECOMMENDATIONS

Begin by organizing your observations and feedback according to the *Lunch Money* categories:

Time is Money
How efficient is the staff in their breakfast and lunch production? What time management strategies might improve staff processes and save time and money? What training and tools do they need?

Milk Moolah
What kinds of milk are they serving? What are the cost implications?

The Commodity Cash Cow
Are they diverting their commodities to processors? How can they maximize their commodity allotment?

Choice Cuts
How many entrée choices are they offering? How much wasted time and wasted food result from the current menu? Are they maximizing economies of scale? Can reducing the menu offerings save them money?

Packaging Pennies
Where are they wasting money on unnecessary packaging, individual servings, or disposable items? What solutions could save money and labor time?

Produce Loot
How cost effective is their method of serving fruits and vegetables? How could a simple salad bar set-up improve the food quality of the food they serve and reduce their labor time?

Breakfast Bucks

Are they maximizing profits from breakfast service? To what degree would a breakfast in the classroom program benefit their bottom line?

Bean Counting

Is the staff serving canned beans or dried beans? What are the cost implications?

Waste Not, Want Not

Are they wasting food and money due to unnecessary trim loss or overproduction?

Sweet Dough

How does dessert factor into their profits? What problems does it pose? What are other options? Are they really generating a significant profit from à la carte sales?

Taking Stock

Do they know what stock they have on hand, what it's worth, and when they intend to use it? How can they improve their current inventory system and how might that save them money?

Fork It Over

Are they using disposable flatware? Do they know what it's costing them? Would they be able to pay someone to wash reusable flatware with the money saved over the course of a school year? How can they create a cafeteria environment that both saves them money and teaches their students to be environmentally responsible?

As you identify areas for improvement, how will you present your suggestions in a way that motivates and inspires the food service director to believe that change is possible, affordable, and necessary?

How can you deliver your feedback in a way that nurtures the development of a school food culture that believes scratch-cooked, whole foods served in schools is the solution to ensuring that children have the healthy and productive lives they deserve?

✔ **NOTE:** *The corresponding "A Getting Started Checklist" worksheet for use in your own district can be found in Part V, Tools of the Trade, Worksheet #1.*

Tools Of The Trade

PART V

Tools Of The Trade

My grandfather – like many grandfathers – used to tell me, "You can't do a good job without the right tools."

In this section, you will find useful worksheets and diagrams to help you put the lessons you have learned in *Lunch Money* to work for you.

WORKSHEET #1
A GETTING STARTED CHECKLIST

FINDING MONEY IN YOUR FOOD SERVICE OPERATIONS

After reading *Lunch Money*, you should be able to begin analyzing your own operations and create a plan for positive change. Use the following categories to conduct your own informal audit to identify the hidden money in your operations that can help pay for your transformation to scratch-cooking.

☐ **Time is Money**
How efficient is our staff in breakfast and lunch production?
What time management strategies might improve staff processes and save time and money?
What training and tools do we need?

☐ **Milk Moolah**
What kinds of milk are being served?
What are the cost implications?

☐ **The Commodity Cash Cow**
Are commodities being diverted to processors?
How can our commodity allotment be maximized?

☐ **Choice Cuts**
How many entrée choices are we offering?
How much wasted time and food results from the current menu?
Are we maximizing economies of scale?
Can reducing the menu offerings save us money?

☐ **Packaging Pennies**
Where are we wasting money on unnecessary packaging, individual servings, or disposable items?
What solutions could save money and labor time?

☐ **Produce Loot**
How cost effective is our method of serving fruits and vegetables?
How could a simple salad bar set-up improve the food quality of the food we serve and reduce our labor time?

☐ **Breakfast Bucks**
Are we maximizing profits from breakfast service?
To what degree would a breakfast in the classroom program benefit our bottom line?

☐ **Bean Counting**
Is the staff serving canned beans or dried beans?
What are the cost implications?

☐ **Waste Not, Want Not**
Are we wasting food and money due to unnecessary trim loss or overproduction?

☐ **Sweet Dough**
How does dessert factor into our profits?
What problems does it pose?
What are other options?
Are we really generating a significant profit from à la carte sales?

- ☐ **Taking Stock**
  Do we know what stock we have on hand, what it's worth, and when we intend to use it?
  How can we improve our current inventory system and how might that save us money?

- ☐ **Fork It Over**
  Are we using disposable flatware?
  Do we know what it's costing us?
  Would we be able to hire someone to wash reusable flatware with the money saved over the course of a school year?
  How can we create a cafeteria environment that both saves us money and teaches our students to be environmentally responsible?

As you identify areas for improvement, consider how you will introduce these changes in a way that motivates and inspires your staff to believe that change is possible, affordable, and necessary. Embrace significant change as a way to nurture the development of a school food culture that believes scratch-cooked, whole foods served in schools is the solution to ensuring that our children have the healthy and productive lives they deserve.

WORKSHEET #2
A PENNY SAVED IS A PENNY EARNED

HOW THIS WORKSHEET WORKS: *Use this worksheet to determine how much money your district would save in a single school year if you were to save one cent on each meal you serve.*

CALCULATING THE VALUE OF A PENNY

1.	Number of meals served in your district per school day		__________
2.	Number of school days per year	x	__________
3.	Number of meals served in your district per school year *(Multiply Line 1 by Line 2, above)*		__________
4.	Multiply by a penny	x	$ .01
5.	**Total saved per year by saving one penny per meal**		$ __________

Applying the principles and formulas you learn in *Lunch Money* will help you identify areas in your own school food service operation where you can increase revenue and decrease expenses — money that can be used to fund scratch-cooked school meals.

WORKSHEET #3
SWEET DOUGH

HOW THIS WORKSHEET WORKS: *Use this worksheet to determine how much money your district would save in a single school year if you were to eliminate serving desserts.*

CALCULATING THE COST SAVINGS OF ELIMINATING DESSERTS

STEP ONE CALCULATE THE NUMBER OF SERVINGS OF DESSERT SERVED PER SCHOOL YEAR

1. Number of servings of dessert served per day		__________
2. Number of days per week dessert is served	x	__________
3. Number of servings of dessert served per week *(Multiply line 1 by line 2, above)*		__________
4. Number of weeks per school year that dessert is served	x	__________
5. Number of Servings of Dessert Served per School Year		__________

STEP TWO CALCULATE AMOUNT OF MONEY SAVED BY ELIMINATING DESSERT

6. Number of servings of dessert served per school year *(Insert from line 5, above)*		__________
7. Food cost per serving of dessert	x	$ __________
8. Savings Per School Year by Eliminating Dessert		$ __________

WORKSHEET #4
MILK MOOLAH

HOW THIS WORKSHEET WORKS: *Use this worksheet to help you determine how much money your district would save by serving only unflavored milk.*

CALCULATING THE COST OF FLAVORED MILK

STEP ONE CALCULATE THE NUMBER OF SERVINGS OF FLAVORED MILK SERVED PER SCHOOL YEAR

1.	Average number of cartons of flavored milk served per meal period		________
2.	Number of times flavored milk is served per week	x	________
3.	Number of cartons of flavored milk served per week *(Multiply line 1 by line 2, above)*		________
4.	Number of weeks per school year that flavored milk is served	x	________
5.	**Number of Cartons of Flavored Milk Served per School Year** *(Multiply line 3 by line 4, above)*		________

WORKSHEET #4 MILK MOOLAH

DIFFERENCE IN COST BETWEEN FLAVORED AND UNFLAVORED MILK

STEP TWO CALCULATE THE PREMIUM PRICE PER CARTON OF FLAVORED MILK

6.	Price per case of flavored milk		$
7.	Price per case of unflavored milk	–	$
8.	Premium price paid per case of flavored milk *(Subtract line 7 from line 6, above)*		$
9.	Number of cartons of milk per case	÷	
10.	**Premium Price per Carton of Flavored Milk** *(Divide line 8 by line 9, above)*		$

STEP THREE CALCULATE AMOUNT OF MONEY SAVED PER YEAR BY SERVING ONLY UNFLAVORED MILK

11.	Number of Cartons of Flavored Milk Served per School Year *(Insert from line 5, above)*		
12.	Premium Price per Carton of Flavored Milk *(Insert from line 10, above)*	x	$
13.	**Amount of Money Saved per Year by Serving Only Unflavored Milk** *(Multiply line 11 by line 12, above)*		$

WORKSHEET #4 MILK MOOLAH

MORE MILK MATH . . .

HOW THIS WORKSHEET WORKS: *Use this worksheet to calculate how much added sugar your district's student body will consume each year as a result of serving flavored milk.*

CALCULATING THE ADDED SUGARS IN FLAVORED MILK:

ADDED SUGARS IN A SERVING OF FLAVORED MILK

STEP ONE CALCULATE THE NUMBER OF ADDED GRAMS OF SUGARS PER 8 OZ CARTON OF FLAVORED MILK

1. Total number of grams of sugars in an 8 oz carton of flavored milk ________ g
2. Total number of grams of sugars in an 8 oz carton of unflavored milk – ________ g
3. **Total number of added grams of sugars in each 8 oz carton of flavored milk** ________ **g**
   (Subtract line 2 from line 1, above)

STEP TWO CALCULATE THE NUMBER OF TEASPOONS OF ADDED SUGARS PER 8 OZ CARTON OF FLAVORED MILK

4. Total number of added grams of sugars in each 8 oz carton of flavored milk ________
5. Number of grams of sugars per teaspoon ÷ 4.2 g
6. **Total number of teaspoons of added sugars per 8 oz carton of flavored milk** ________ **tsp**
   (Divide line 4 by line 5, above)

WORKSHEET #4 MILK MOOLAH

ADDED SUGARS IN A YEAR'S WORTH OF FLAVORED MILK

STEP THREE CALCULATE THE NUMBER OF TEASPOONS OF ADDED SUGARS PER SCHOOL YEAR FOR A CHILD DRINKING FLAVORED MILK

7. Total number of teaspoons of added sugars per 8 oz carton of flavored milk ________ tsp
(Insert total from line 6, above)

8. Number of school days per year x ________

9. Number of times per school day that flavored milk is offered x ________

10. Total number of teaspoons of added sugars per school year for a child drinking flavored milk for both breakfast and lunch ________ tsp
(Multiply the amounts in lines 7, 8, and 9, above)

STEP FOUR CALCULATE THE NUMBER OF POUNDS OF ADDED SUGARS PER SCHOOL YEAR FOR A CHILD DRINKING FLAVORED MILK

11. Total number of teaspoons of added sugars per school year for a child drinking flavored milk for both breakfast and lunch ________ tsp
(Insert total from line 10, above)

12. Approximate number of teaspoons of sugars per pound ÷ 115 tsp

13. Total number of pounds of added sugars per school year for a child drinking flavored milk ________ lbs

WORKSHEET #5
BEAN COUNTING

HOW THIS WORKSHEET WORKS: *Use this worksheet to calculate how much money your district can save by switching from canned to dried beans.*

CALCULATING THE SAVINGS FROM SWITCHING TO DRIED BEANS

BEAN YIELDS CHART		
VARIETY	CANNED USDA Recommended Drained Weight (Minimum in Ounces per #10 Can)	DRIED 1 Pound Raw Yields This Number of Pounds Cooked*
Garbanzo Beans	68 oz	2.2 lbs
Kidney Beans	68 oz	2.6 lbs
Pinto Beans	68 oz	2.8 lbs

* Source: *The Book of Yields: Accuracy in Food Costing and Purchasing*, by Francis T. Lynch.

CALCULATING THE COST OF CANNED KIDNEY BEANS

STEP ONE CALCULATE YIELD OF CANNED KIDNEY BEANS

1. Drained weight per #10 can of kidney beans ________ oz
2. Number of # 10 cans per case x ________
3. **Ounces per Case of Drained Canned Kidney Beans** ________ **oz**
   (Multiply Line 1 by Line 2, above)

WORKSHEET #5 BEAN COUNTING

STEP TWO CALCULATE PRICE PER POUND OF CANNED KIDNEY BEANS

4.	Price per case of canned kidney beans		$ ________
5.	Number of ounces per case of canned kidney beans *(Insert from Line 3, above)*	÷	________ oz
6.	Price per ounce of canned kidney beans *(Divide Line 4 by Line 5, above)*		$ ________ per oz
7.	Number of ounces per pound	x	16 oz per lb
8.	**Price per Pound of Canned Kidney Beans** *(Multiply Line 6 by Line 7, above)*		**$ ________ per lb**

CALCULATING THE COST OF DRIED KIDNEY BEANS

STEP THREE CALCULATE YIELD OF DRIED KIDNEY BEANS

9.	Yield of 1 pound of dried kidney beans after cooking		________ lbs
10.	Number of pounds of dried kidney beans per case	x	________
11.	**Total Pounds of Kidney Beans per Case of Dried Beans After Cooking** *(Multiply Line 9 by Line 10, above)*		**________ lbs**

STEP FOUR CALCULATE PRICE PER POUND OF DRIED KIDNEY BEANS

12.	Price per case of dried kidney beans		$ ________ per case
13.	Number of pounds of kidney beans per case of dried beans after cooking *(Insert from Line 11, above)*	÷	________ lbs
14.	**Price per Pound of Cooked Dried Beans** *(Divide Line 12 by Line 13)*		**$ ________ per lb**

WORKSHEET #5 BEAN COUNTING

CALCULATING THE DIFFERENCE BETWEEN DRIED AND CANNED KIDNEY BEANS

STEP FIVE CALCULATE DIFFERENCE IN PRICE PER POUND OF CANNED BEANS VERSUS PRICE OF DRIED BEANS

15. Price per pound of canned kidney beans — $ ______ per lb
    (Insert from Line 8, above)

16. Price per pound of cooked dried beans — – $ ______ per lb
    (Insert from Line 14, above)

17. **Savings per Pound by Serving Dried Beans Versus Canned Beans:** — **$ ______ saved per lb**
    (Line 15 minus Line 16, above)

STEP SIX CALCULATE MONEY SAVED EACH SCHOOL YEAR BY SERVING DRIED BEANS VERSUS CANNED BEANS

18. Number of lunches served per day — ______ servings per day

19. Number of 2 oz servings per pound of beans — ÷ ______ servings per lb

20. Number of pounds of beans needed — ______ lbs per day served
    (Divide Line 18 by Line 19, above)

21. Number of school weeks per year — x ______ weeks per school year

22. Number of pounds of beans used per school year (served 1 day per week) — ______ lbs per school year
    (Multiply Line 20 by Line 21, above)

23. Savings per pound by serving dried beans versus canned beans — x $ ______ lb saved
    (Insert from Line 17, above)

24. **Savings per Year by Serving Dried Beans Versus Canned Beans** — **$ ______ saved per year**
    (Multiply Line 22 by Line 23, above)

WORKSHEET #6
FORK IT OVER

HOW THIS WORKSHEET WORKS: *Use this worksheet to calculate your potential cost savings by switching from disposable to reusable flatware.*

CALCULATING THE COST SAVINGS OF REPLACING DISPOSABLE WITH REUSABLE FLATWARE

(Note: "Forks" is used throughout this worksheet, but it can also be used for spoons, knives, and even styrofoam trays.)

CALCULATING THE COST OF DISPOSABLE FORKS

STEP ONE CALCULATE THE NUMBER OF DISPOSABLE FORKS USED PER SCHOOL YEAR

1. Number of lunches served per day ____________
2. Number of breakfasts served per day + ____________
3. Total number of meals served per day ____________
   (Add lines 1 and 2, above)
4. Number of disposable forks used per meal x ____________
5. Number of disposable forks used per day ____________
   (Multiply line 3 by line 4, above)
6. Number of days per school year x ____________
7. **Number of disposable forks used per School Year** ____________
   (Multiply line 5 by line 6, above)

WORKSHEET #6 FORK IT OVER

STEP TWO CALCULATE THE COST OF DISPOSABLE FORKS PER SCHOOL YEAR

6.	Number of disposable forks used per school year *(Insert from line 5, above)*		______
7.	Cost per disposable fork	x	$ ______ ea
8.	**Cost for disposable forks per school year** *(Multiply line 6 by line 7, above)*		$ ______

CALCULATING THE COST OF REUSABLE FORKS

STEP THREE CALCULATE THE NUMBER OF REUSABLE FORKS NEEDED PER SCHOOL YEAR

9.	Total number of meals served per day *(Insert from line 3, above)*		______
10.	Number of reusable forks used per meal	x	______
11.	**Total number of reusable forks needed per year** *(Multiply line 9 by line 10, above)*		______

STEP FOUR CALCULATE THE COST OF REUSABLE FORKS PER SCHOOL YEAR

12.	Cost per case of reusable forks		$ ______ cs
13.	Number of reusable forks per case	÷	______
14.	Cost per disposable fork *(Divide line 12 by line 13, above)*		$ ______ ea
15.	Total number of reusable forks needed per year *(Insert from line 11, above)*	x	______
16.	**Cost for reusable per school year**		$ ______

WORKSHEET #6 FORK IT OVER

CALCULATING THE COST SAVINGS OF SWITCHING TO REUSABLE FORKS

STEP FIVE CALCULATE THE COST SAVINGS PER SCHOOL YEAR OF SWITCHING TO REUSABLE FORKS

17.	Cost for disposable forks per school year *(Insert from line 8, above)*		$ ________
18.	Cost for reusable forks per school year	–	$ ________
19.	**Cost Savings Per School Year of Switching to Reusable Forks** *(Subtract line 18 from line 17, above)*		**$** ________

WORKSHEET #7
BIG BREAKFAST BUCKS

HOW THIS WORKSHEET WORKS: *Use this worksheet to calculate your potential increase in net revenue if you were to shift from serving breakfast in the cafeteria to serving breakfast in the classroom.*

MEAL, SNACK AND MILK PAYMENTS TO STATES AND SCHOOL FOOD AUTHORITIES *Expressed in Dollars or Fractions Thereof. Effective from July 1, 2011 through June 30, 2012*			
SCHOOL BREAKFAST PROGRAM		**NON-SEVERE NEED**	**SEVERE NEED**
Contiguous States	Paid	.27	.27
	Reduced Price	1.21	1.50
	Free	1.51	1.80
Alaska	Paid	.40	.40
	Reduced Price	2.11	2.58
	Free	2.41	2.88
Hawaii	Paid	.30	.30
	Reduced Price	1.46	1.80
	Free	1.76	2.10

CALCULATING POTENTIAL ADDITIONAL NET REVENUE FROM BIC PROGRAM
DETERMINE YOUR CONSTANTS FOR THE YEAR
STEP ONE DETERMINE STUDENT ELIGIBILITY

1. Total number of students eligible for free meals __________
2. Total number of students eligible for reduced meals __________
3. Total number of students not eligible for either free or reduced-price meals __________
4. **Total Number of Students** __________
   (Add lines 1, 2 and 3, above)

WORKSHEET #7 BIG BREAKFAST BUCKS

STEP TWO DETERMINE CURRENT AVERAGE DAILY PARTICIPATION

5. Average daily number of students eligible for free meals who eat breakfast ________
6. Average daily number of students eligible for reduced meals who eat breakfast ________
7. Average daily number of students not eligible for either free or reduced-price meals who eat breakfast ________
8. **Total Number of Students Currently Participating in Breakfast Program** ________
   (Add lines 5, 6, and 7, above)

STEP THREE DETERMINE YOUR SALES PRICES

9. Price paid for breakfast by students eligible for free meals $________
10. Price paid for breakfast by students eligible for reduced-price meals $________
11. Price paid for breakfast by students not eligible for either free or reduced-price meals $________

STEP FOUR DETERMINE REIMBURSEMENT RATES

12. **Free**

    (a) Federal reimbursement rate for students eligible for free breakfast $________
    (For districts that served 40% or more free or reduced-price lunches during the 2009-2010 school year, insert $1.80; all others insert $1.51.)

    (b) State reimbursement rate for students eligible for free breakfast $ 0.00

    (c) Other reimbursements for students eligible for free breakfast $ 0.00
    (Note: Do not include cash sales on this line.)

    (d) Total Reimbursements for Students Eligible for Free Breakfast $________
    (Add lines 12(a), 12(b) and 12(c), above)

WORKSHEET #7 BIG BREAKFAST BUCKS

13. **Reduced**

(a) Federal reimbursement rate for students eligible for reduced-price breakfast $ ________

(For districts that served 40% or more free or reduced-price lunches during 2009-2010 school year, insert $1.50; all others insert $1.21.)

(b) State reimbursement rate for students eligible for reduced-price breakfast $ ________

(c) Other reimbursements for students eligible for reduced-price breakfast $ ________

(Note: Do not include cash sales on this line.)

(d) Total Reimbursements for Students Eligible for Reduced-Price Breakfast $ ________

(Add lines 13(a), 13(b) and 13(c), above)

14. **Paid**

(a) Federal reimbursement rate for students not eligible for either free or reduced-price breakfast $ .27

(All districts insert $ .27.)

(b) State reimbursement rate for students not eligible for either free or reduced-price breakfast $ ________

(c) Other reimbursement rate for students not eligible for either free or reduced-price breakfast $ ________

(Note: Do not include cash sales on this line.)

(d) Total Reimbursements for Students Not Eligible for Either Free or Reduced-Price Breakfast $ ________

(Add lines 14(a), 14(b) and 14(c), above)

WORKSHEET #7 BIG BREAKFAST BUCKS

STEP FIVE DETERMINE FOOD COST PER MEAL

15. Average Daily Food Cost per Meal for Breakfast $______

STEP SIX
DETERMINE NUMBER OF DAYS PER SCHOOL YEAR

16. Number of Days per School Year on which Breakfast is Served ______

CALCULATE POTENTIAL NET REVENUE FROM BREAKFAST IN THE CLASSROOM

STEP SEVEN CALCULATE POTENTIAL REIMBURSEMENTS PER DAY

17. Total potential reimbursements for students eligible for free breakfast $______
    (Multiply line 1 (_____) by line 12(d) (_____), above)
18. Total potential reimbursements for students eligible for reduced-price breakfast $______
    (Multiply line 2 (_____) by line 13(d) (_____), above)
19. Total potential reimbursements for students not eligible for either free or reduced-price breakfast $______
    (Multiply line 3 (_____) by line 14(d) (_____), above)
20. **Total Potential Reimbursements per Day** $______
    (Add lines 17, 18, and 19, above)

STEP EIGHT CALCULATE POTENTIAL TOTAL FOOD COST PER DAY FOR BREAKFAST

21. **Total Potential Food Cost Per Day for Breakfast** $______
    (Multiply line 4 (_____) by line 15 (_____), above)

WORKSHEET #7 BIG BREAKFAST BUCKS

STEP NINE CALCULATE POTENTIAL NET REVENUE FROM BREAKFAST IN THE CLASSROOM PER DAY

22. Total Potential Daily Net Revenue from Breakfast in the Classroom $ ________
(Subtract line 21 from line 20, above)

STEP TEN CALCULATE POTENTIAL NET REVENUE FROM BREAKFAST IN THE CLASSROOM PER SCHOOL YEAR

23. Number of school days per year on which breakfast is served x ________
(Insert from line 16, above)

24. Total Potential Annual Net Revenue from Breakfast in the Classroom $ ________
(Multiply line 22 (_____) by line 23 (_____), above)

CALCULATE NET REVENUE FOR CURRENT BREAKFAST PROGRAM

STEP ELEVEN CALCULATE CURRENT REIMBURSEMENTS FROM BREAKFAST IN THE CAFETERIA PER DAY

25. Total current reimbursements for students eligible for free breakfast $ ________
(Multiply line 5 (_____) by line 12(d) (_____), above)

26. Total current reimbursements for students eligible for reduced-price breakfast $ ________
(Multiply line 6 (_____) by line 13(d) (_____), above)

27. Total current reimbursements for students not eligible for either free or reduced-price breakfast $ ________
(Multiply line 7 (_____) by line 14(d) (_____), above)

28. Total Current Reimbursements from Breakfast per Day $ ________
(Add lines 25, 26 and 27, above)

WORKSHEET #7 BIG BREAKFAST BUCKS

STEP TWELVE CALCULATE CURRENT REVENUE FROM SALES OF BREAKFAST PER DAY

29. Total current daily revenue from sales of breakfast to students eligible for free breakfast $______
(Multiply line 5 (____) by line 9 (____), above)

30. Total current daily revenue from sales of breakfast to students eligible for reduced-price breakfast $______
(Multiply line 6 (____) by line 10 (____), above)

31. Total current daily revenue from sales of breakfast to students not eligible for either free or reduced-price breakfast $______
(Multiply line 7 (____) by line 11 (____), above)

32. **Total Current Revenues from Sales of Breakfast per day** $______
(Add lines 29, 30 and 31, above)

STEP THIRTEEN CALCULATE TOTAL CURRENT REVENUE FROM BREAKFAST SALES AND REIMBURSEMENTS PER DAY

33. Total current reimbursements from breakfast per day $______
(Insert from line 28, above)

34. Total current revenues from sales of breakfast per day $______
(Insert from line 32, above)

35. **Total Current Revenue from Breakfast Sales and Reimbursements per Day** $______
(Add lines 33 and 34, above)

STEP FOURTEEN CALCULATE TOTAL CURRENT FOOD COST FOR BREAKFAST PER DAY

36. **Total Current Food Cost for Breakfast per Day** $______
(Multiply line 8 (____) by line 15 (____), above)

WORKSHEET #7 BIG BREAKFAST BUCKS

STEP FIFTEEN CALCULATE CURRENT NET REVENUE FROM BREAKFAST PER DAY

37. **Current Net Revenue from Breakfast per Day** $ ________
(Subtract line 36 from line 35, above)

STEP SIXTEEN CALCULATE CURRENT NET REVENUE FROM BREAKFAST PER SCHOOL YEAR

38. Number of school days per year on which breakfast is served x ________
(Insert from line 16, above)

39. **Total Current Annual Net Revenue from breakfast in the cafeteria** $ ________
(Multiply line 37 (______) by line 38 (_____), above)

COMPARE POTENTIAL NET REVENUE FOR BIC PROGRAM TO REVENUE FOR CURRENT BREAKFAST PROGRAM

STEP SEVENTEEN CALCULATE POTENTIAL ADDITIONAL NET REVENUE FROM BREAKFAST IN THE CLASSROOM PER SCHOOL YEAR

40. Total potential annual net revenue from breakfast in the classroom $ ________
(Insert from line 24, above)

41. Total current annual net revenue from breakfast in the cafeteria – $ ________
(Insert from line 39, above)

42. **Potential Additional Net Revenue per School Year from Switching to a Breakfast in the Classroom Program** $ ________
(Subtract line 41 from line 40, above)

WORKSHEET #7 BIG BREAKFAST BUCKS

A NOTE ABOUT LABOR TIME: *As mentioned earlier, it is important to note that labor and overhead expenses rarely increase with the introduction of a Breakfast in the Classroom program in a school that is already offering breakfast in the cafeteria. Where Breakfast in the Classroom is being added to a school in which breakfast was not previously offered at all, additional labor costs may result. In those cases, the total additional labor cost for the year should be subtracted from line 42 for an accurate calculation of Potential Additional Net Revenue from Breakfast in the Classroom.*

WORKSHEET #8
CYCLE MENU PLANNING CALENDAR

CYCLE MENU PLANNING CALENDAR					
THEME					
WEEK	MONDAY	TUESDAY	WEDNESDAY	THURSDAY	FRIDAY
1					
2					
3					
4					

WORKSHEET #9
INVENTORY ON HAND RECORD

INVENTORY ON HAND RECORD

DATE:
SITE:
STORAGE LOCATION: ____________________

ITEM	UNIT OF MEASURE	PAR STOCK	NUMBER OF UNITS ON HAND	X	COST PER UNIT	=	VALUE ON HAND
				X	$	=	$
				X	$	=	$
				X	$	=	$
				X	$	=	$
				X	$	=	$
				X	$	=	$
				X	$	=	$
				X	$	=	$
				X	$	=	$
				X	$	=	$
				X	$	=	$
				X	$		$
				X	$		$
				X	$	=	$

WORKSHEET #10
INVENTORY USE RECORD

INVENTORY USE RECORD

DATE:
SITE:
STORAGE LOCATION: ______________________

ITEM	UNIT OF MEASURE	NUMBER OF UNITS ON HAND AT LAST INVENTORY	+	NUMBER OF UNITS RECEIVED SINCE LAST INVENTORY	−	NUMBER OF UNITS CURRENTLY ON HAND	=	UNITS USED DURING INVENTORY PERIOD
			+		−		=	
			+		−		=	
			+		−		=	
			+		−		=	
			+		−		=	
			+		−		=	
			+		−		=	
			+		−		=	
			+		−		=	
			+		−		=	
			+		−		=	
			+		−		=	
			+		−		=	

WORKSHEET #11
UNDERSTANDING TRIM LOSS

UNDERSTANDING TRIM LOSS

Understanding the concept of "Trim Loss" and its value will encourage you to minimize waste.

"TRIM LOSS" *is the amount of a product that is removed and not used in the production of a specific recipe. For example, when a carrot is peeled before slicing, the peel and the ends are considered the trim and has a dollar value that can be assigned to it.*

Determine the amount of trim loss by weighing the product before doing anything to it (the "as purchased" weight) and weighing it again after you have trimmed and peeled it (the "usable portion"). The difference between the two weights is the amount of trim loss:

As Purchased Weight – Usable Portion Weight = Trim Loss

You can determine the value of your Trim Loss by multiplying the number of pounds of Trim Loss by the price you paid per pound:

Trim Loss in Pounds x Price Paid per Pound = Dollar Value of Trim Loss

EXAMPLE

Imagine that a 50 pound bag of raw carrots costs $62.50, or $1.25 per pound:

$62.50 ÷ 50 lbs = $1.25 per lb

If, after the carrots are peeled, you are left with 45 usable pounds of carrots, the Trim Loss is 5 pounds:

50 lbs – 45 lbs = 5 lbs

At $1.25 per pound, your Trim Loss has a total dollar value of $6.25:

$1.25 per lb x 5 lbs = $6.25 per lb

WORKSHEET #12
UNDERSTANDING YIELD PERCENTAGE

UNDERSTANDING YIELD PERCENTAGE

Knowing how to use Yield Percentage when calculating your food cost will help you stay on budget.

"YIELD PERCENTAGE" *is the percentage of the original product that you can actually use after you've trimmed and peeled it, and is calculated by dividing the Usable Portion Weight by the As Purchased Weight:*

Usable Portion Weight ÷ As Purchased Weight = Yield Percentage

The yield percentage will help you properly cost recipes. To calculate the cost per usable pound, for example, you would divide the Price Paid per Pound As Purchased by the Yield Percentage:

Price Paid per Pound As Purchased ÷ Yield Percentage = Cost per Usable Pound

EXAMPLE

A roasted carrot recipe requires 8 pounds of peeled carrots. Imagine that a 50 pound bag of carrots costs $62.50, or $1.25 per pound ($62.50 ÷ 50 lbs = $1.25 per lb). After the carrots are peeled, you are left with 45 pounds of usable carrots. To determine the actual cost per pound of the usable portion, we use the following two formulas:

1. ***45 lbs Usable Portion Weight ÷ 50 lbs As Purchased Weight = 90% Yield Percentage***
2. ***$1.25 Price Paid per Pound As Purchased ÷ 90% (or .90) Yield Percentage = $1.39 Cost per Usable Pound***

Finally, when calculating the food cost of a recipe calling for a product that involves Trim Loss (such as carrots, onions, potatoes, celery, lettuce), multiply the number of pounds needed for the recipe by the Cost per Usable Pound, not by the Price per Pound as Purchased:

8 lbs x $1.39 = $11.12 food cost for the carrots used in the recipe

Note that if you had failed to take Trim Loss into consideration and calculated your food cost for the recipe using the Price Paid per Pound as Purchased of $1.25, you would have underestimated the cost by $1.12:

8 lbs x $1.25 = $10.00

DIAGRAM #1
SIMPLE SALAD BAR LAYOUT

SALAD GREENS Leaf lettuce, romaine, mesclun, spinach or any mix thereof are good options. Iceberg lettuce should be limited, as it is not as nutrient-dense as other options.

FRESH VEGETABLES Options include broccoli, cauliflower, carrots, tomatoes, bell peppers, cucumbers, celery, fresh green or wax beans, snow peas, sugar snap peas, roasted zucchini or yellow squash, roasted potatoes, hot peppers, mushrooms, jicama, onions, radishes, etc. Cold roasted vegetables may also be used.

FRESH FRUIT Options include apples, oranges, kiwi, bananas, pears, grapes, etc. Before placing fresh fruit on the salad bar, first make sure that it is ripe, and then section it into halves or quarters to help encourage students to take only the portion that they will eat and, with respect to younger children, to help them wrap their small hands and mouths around it.

DIAGRAM #2
COMPLEX SALAD BAR LAYOUT

Romaine Leaf Lettuce Mesclun Spinach	Chicken Turkey Pork	Mozzarella Cheddar Cottage Cheese	Beets Red Cabbage Roasted Eggplant	Peas Corn	Low-Fat Creamy Dressing
	Hardboiled Eggs Tofu Light Tuna	Brocolli Cauliflower	Tomatoes Bell Peppers	Walnuts Almonds Sunflower Seeds Pepitas Pumpkin Seeds	Diced Apples Sliced Pears Citrus Segments Raisins Dried Cranberries Dried Apricots Dried Dates
	Garbanzo Beans Kidney Beans Black Beans Navy Beans Pinto Beans	Carrots	Cucumbers Celery	Other*	Fat-Free Dressing

***OTHER** Can include fresh green or wax beans, snow peas, sugar snap peas, roasted zucchini or yellow squash, roasted potatoes, olives, hot peppers, mushrooms, bean sprouts, jicama, onions, radishes, etc.

ALL PRODUCTS SHOULD BE FRESH EXCEPT: Tuna (canned), legumes (dried or canned), olives (bottled), hot peppers (bottled), peas and corn (frozen). Cheeses are all "lowfat."

NOTE: Diagram assumes a three-well refrigerated table. Pans used are 6" or 4" half and sixth hotel pans. Each pan must be filled with one of the options listed daily. Choices should vary from day to day to the greatest extent possible.

DIAGRAM #3
FLOW OF SERVICE DIAGRAM

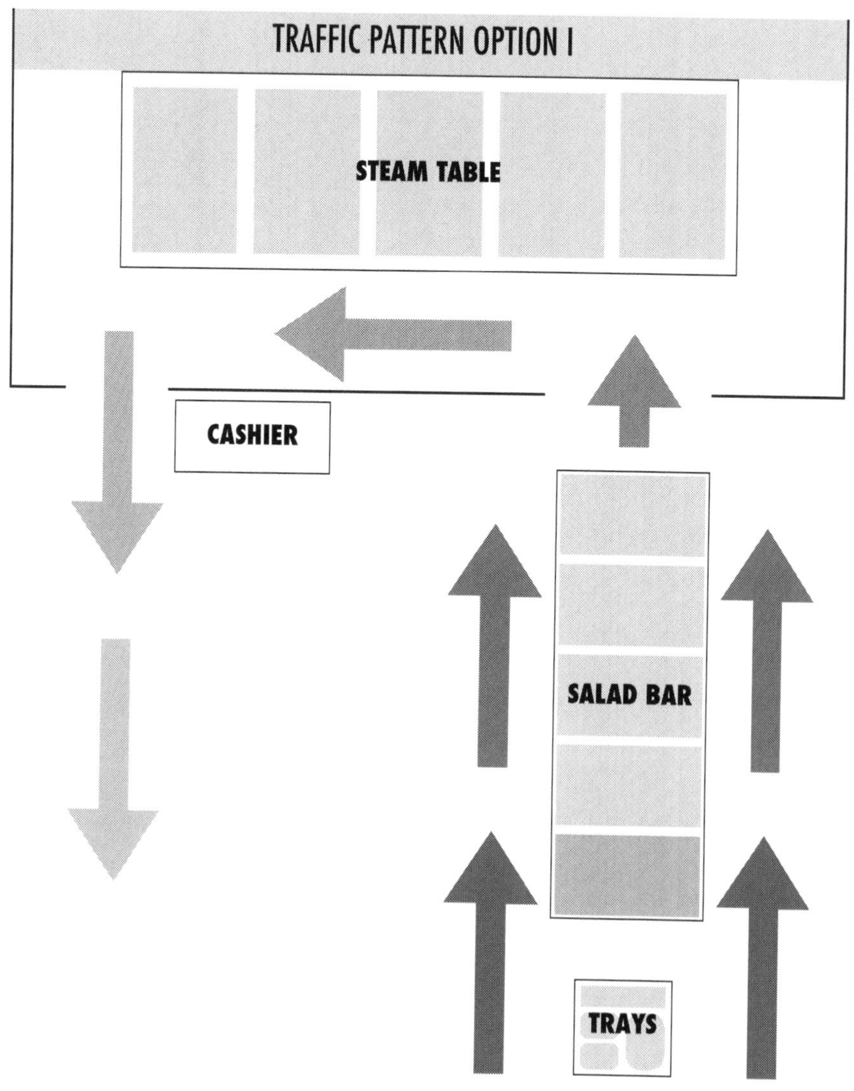

DIAGRAM #4
ALTERNATIVE FLOW OF SERVICE DIAGRAM

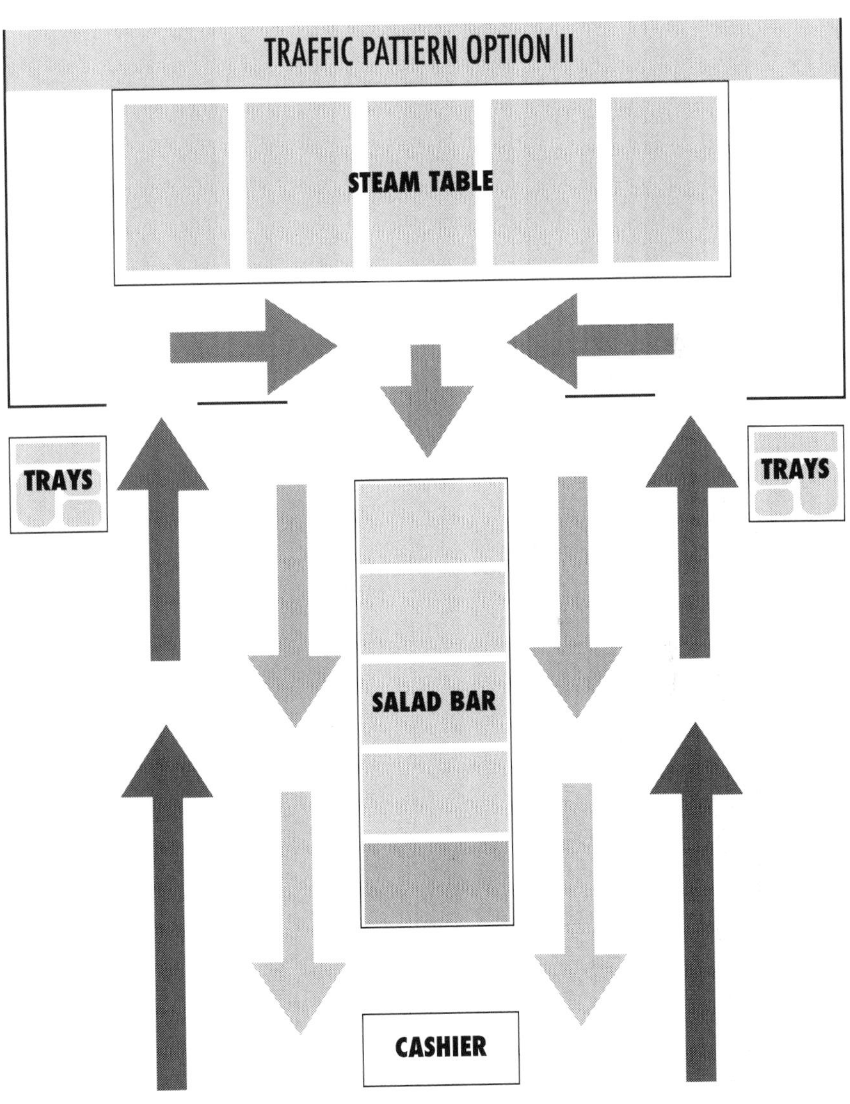

Second Helpings

PART VI

Second Helpings

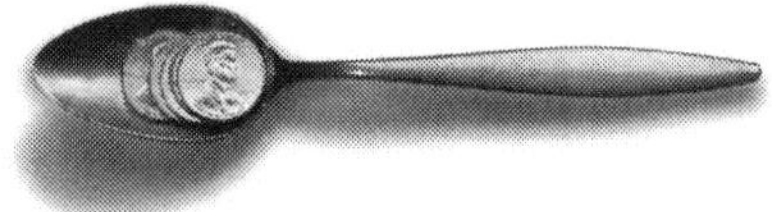

The following is a list of books, websites, blogs, and films that – whether entertaining, polemical, or both – are but a select few of the many useful resources available for those looking for more information about food systems in general and school food in particular.

BOOKS

Animal, Vegetable, Miracle: A Year of Food Life, by Barbara Kingsolver, is an entertaining nonfiction narrative about the popular author's year of feeding herself and her family for a year solely with food grown in their own neighborhood. HarperCollins (2007).

Appetite for Profit: How the Food Industry Undermines our Health and How to Fight Back, by Michele Simon, offers solid advice from its attorney author about how to fight back against the powerful food and beverage industry. Nation Books (2006).

The Book of Yields: Accuracy in Food Costing and Purchasing, by Francis T. Lynch, is every savvy chef's resource for determining food cost, weight-to-volume equivalents, trim yields, and cooking yields. John Wiley & Sons (8th edition, 2010).

Don't Eat This Book: Fast Food and the Supersizing of America, by Morgan Spurlock, is the author's good-humored explanation of the sad consequences of America's predilection for fast food. Berkley Trade (2006).

The End of Overeating: Taking Control of the Insatiable American Appetite, by Dr. David Kessler, describes overating as "a biological challenge, not a character flaw," blaming the ubiquitous availability of fat, sugar, and salt in the American diet as the culprit in the national obesity crisis. Rodale Books (2009).

Fast Food Nation, by Eric Schlosser, describes the destructive effect of America's fast food culture on the environment, the economy, the labor force, and the health of our nation. Houghton Mifflin (2001).

Fed Up with Lunch: The School Lunch Project: How One Anonymous Teacher Revealed the Truth About School Lunches – And How We Can Change Them!, by Sarah Wu, describes the journey of Chicago public school teacher and blogger "Mrs. Q" as she eats school lunch for a year. Chronicle Books (2011).

Food Politics, by Marion Nestle, is a trailblazing book for the food systems reform movement, which brought to light food industry marketing practices. University of California Press (2nd edition, 2007).

Food Rules: An Eater's Manual, by Michael Pollan, is an essential collection of bite-sized tips for eating in the modern world. Penguin (2009).

Free for All: Fixing School Food in America, by Jan Poppendieck, makes a convincing evidence-based case for free school meals for every American student. University of California Press (2011).

How to Cook Everything, by Mark Bittman, is often described as the one cookbook to own if you can only own one. John Wiley & Sons (2nd edition, 2008).

In Defense of Food: An Eater's Manifesto, by Michael Pollan, expounds on Pollan's basic advice to eaters: "Eat food. Not too much. Mostly plants." Penguin (2009).

Keys to Good Cooking: A Guide to Making the Best of Foods and Recipes, by Harold McGee, demystifies the science of cooking and provides practical tips for achieving perfection in the kitchen. Penguin (2010).

Little House in the Big Woods, by Laura Ingalls Wilder, tells the tale of a young girl's family and their daily work to hunt and gather their own food in mid-19th century Wisconsin. HarperCollins (75th Anniversary edition, 2007).

Lunch Lessons: Changing the Way We Feed Our Children, by Ann Cooper and Lisa Holmes, describes the school food reform efforts of dozens of advocates around the country. William Morrow (2006).

Lunch Wars: How to Start a School Food Revolution and Win the Battle for Our Children's Health, by Amy Kalafa, is a guidebook for parents who want to create a school food revolution in their own district. Tarcher (2011).

The Omnivore's Dilemma: A Natural History of Four Meals, by Michael Pollan, is the national bestseller that tells the story of the modern American food chain and its consequences for both producers and consumers. Penguin (2007).

School Lunch Politics: The Surprising History of America's Favorite Welfare Program, by Susan Levine, describes the political influence of private economic interests on a social welfare program intended to address children's nutritional needs. Princeton University Press (2010).

What to Eat, by Marion Nestle, is a comprehensive yet accessible guide to making informed choices about food. North Point Press (2007).

A FEW BOOKS SPECIFICALLY FOR TEACHERS AND STUDENTS

Chew on This: Everything You Don't Want to Know about Fast Food, by Eric Schlosser, is a funny and accessible adaptation of Schlosser's book *Fast Food Nation* written specifically with middle school students in mind. Houghton Mifflin (2007).

How to Teach Nutrition to Kids, by Connie Liakos Evers, is a guide for teachers and parents on integrating healthy eating into other life lessons for children. 24 Carrot Press (3rd edition, 2006).

The Monster Health Book: A Guide to Eating Healthy, Being Active & Feeling Great for Monsters & Kids!, by Edward Miller, is filled with factoids for 2nd through 5th graders about nutrients, calories, and food labels, with a few cooking tips tossed in. Holiday House (2006).

The Omnivore's Dilemma for Kids: The Secrets Behind What You Eat, by Michael Pollan, is Pollan's bestseller of the same title adapted for the young reader. Dial Press (2009).

The Vegetables We Eat, by Gail Gibbons, targets the "picture crowd" in the lower elementary school grades with brightly colored artwork and interesting food facts. Holiday House (2007).

WEBSITES & BLOGS

www.TheAtlantic.com/life/category/food is *The Atlantic* magazine's online blog with entries by some of America's most insightful chefs and food systems thinkers.

www.BetterSchoolFood.org is an online resource for activist parents slated to be repopulated with updated information in early 2012.

www.CivilEats.com is a comprehensive site that "promotes critical thought about sustainable agriculture and food systems as part of building economically and socially just communities" through the writings of more than 100 contributors.

www.Ecoliteracy.org is the website of Zenobia Barlow's renowned Center for Ecoliteracy, which houses free resources for food systems activists including the *Rethinking School Lunch* series and the stunningly beautiful *Cooking with California Food in K-12 Schools* by Georgeanne Brennan and Ann M. Evans.

www.FedUpWithLunch.com is the blog created by Chicago public school teacher and blogger Sarah Wu (also known as "Mrs. Q") providing a daily photo documentary of school lunch.

www.FoodPolitics.com is famed nutritionist and NYU professor Marion Nestle's daily blog documenting her wise and witty insights about current events in the intersecting worlds of food and politics.

www.Grist.org/food is an online source for essays and opinions addressing the relationship between the modern food system and the environment, and describes itself as "a beacon in the smog."

www.jamieoliver.com/us/foundation/jamies-food-revolution is Chef Jamie Oliver's online resource for school food reform activists of all ages.

www.TheLunchTray.com is a daily blog by attorney and mom Bettina Elias Siegal focusing on feeding kids, in schools and out.

www.ParentEarth.com is a social enterprise site devoted to providing educational videos about food to families.

www.RealTimeFarms.com is a go-to site to identify farms, farmers markets, food artisans, and restaurants around the country.

www.TheSlowCook.com is former *Washington Post* reporter Ed Bruske's record of his ceaseless efforts and the efforts of others to ensure that school food is real food.

FILMS

Food Inc. (2008) is an Academy Award nominated documentary that "exposes the highly mechanized underbelly" of the American food system and the interrelationship between the food industry that produces much of our food and the government agencies that regulate them. Featuring Eric Schlosser, Michael Pollan, and Joel Salatin.

King Corn (2007) is a an entertaining and educational documentary that tells the tale of two friends determined to understand the driving forces behind, and the consequences of, subsidized corn in America. Featuring Curt Ellis and Ian Cheney.

Nourish (2009) is an award-winning PBS film that explores our relationship to food. Narrated by Cameron Diaz.

Super Size Me (2004) is an Academy Award nominated film that documents the physiological and psychological consequences of a 30-day fast food diet. Featuring Morgan Spurlock and Alexandra Jamieson. Spurlock subsequently published a companion book to the film entitled, *Supersized: Strange Tales from a Fast-Food Culture*. Dark Horse (2011).

The Future of Food (2004) is Deborah Koons Garcia's exposé of genetic engineering of food and the corporate conglomerates that appear to stop at nothing to ensure the steady propagation of GMO crops.

Two Angry Moms (2007) is a "part exposé, part 'how-to'" film about two angry moms in pursuit of an alternative to the highly processed fare served by the food service management companies in their school districts. Featuring Amy Kalafa and Susan Rubin.

What's On Your Plate (2009) is Catherine Gund's charming documentary that tells the story of two tweens as they journey through city and country to learn where their food comes from. Featuring Sadie and Safiyah.

PART VII

No Reservations

When we started down this road together, we recognized that winning the battle against childhood obesity and diet-related illness will require schools to become part of the solution by serving healthy scratch-cooked meals.

After reading *Lunch Money*, you should have no reservations about calling on your newly-acquired knowledge to begin identifying unnecessary expenses and previously uncaptured revenue in your own school's food service operations. When you put your new skills to work, the money you find will enable you to serve your students healthier and tastier food, provide your food service workers with the culinary training they need, furnish your kitchens with the necessary equipment, and free your district and the students in its care from the misconception that saving money and saving lives cannot coexist. They can. And with your help, they will.

Our children can't afford for you to think that you can't afford it.

"Whether you think you can or think you can't, you're right."
– Henry Ford

NOTES

1 National Center for Health Statistics, Centers for Disease Control and Prevention, U.S. Department of Health and Human Services. "Deaths, Percent of Total Deaths, and Death Rates for the 15 Leading Causes of Death in 5-Year Age Groups, by Race and Sex: United States, 2000." Hyattsville, MD: CDC, 2002.

2 www.thelancet.com. Published online September 6, 2007 DOI:10.1016/S0140-6736(07)61306-3.

3 Wallinga, MD., David, Janelle Sorensen, Pooja, Mottl, Biran Yablon, Md. "Not So Sweet: Missing Mercury and High Fructose Corn Syrup." *Institute for Agriculture and Trade Policy* 2009. Dufault, Renee, Blaise LeBlanc, Roseanne Schnoll, Charles Cornett, Laura Schweitzer, Lyn Patrick, Jane Hightower, David Wallinga, Walter Lukiw. "Mercury from chlor-alkali plants: measured concentrations in food product sugar." *Environmental Health* 2009, 8:2 doi:10.1186/1476-069X-8-2.

4 Centers for Disease Control and Prevention: National Diabetes Fact Sheet: General Information and National Estimates on Diabetes in the United States, 2007. Rev. ed. Atlanta, Ga., *U.S. Department of Health and Human Services, Centers for Disease Control and Prevention*, 2004. One of three (33%) men and nearly 2 of 5 (39%) women born in the United States in 2000 will develop diabetes sometime during their lifetime. For men born in 2000, estimated lifetime risks of developing diabetes were 27% among non-Hispanic whites, 40% among non-Hispanic blacks, and 45% among Hispanics. For women born in 2000, estimated lifetime risks were 31% among non-Hispanic whites, 49% among non-Hispanic blacks, and 53% among Hispanics.

5 *N Engl J Med*, 2005;03/17/05.

6 Federal Interagency Forum on Child and Family Statistics. "America's Children in Brief: Key National Indicators of Well-Being," 2010. Washington, DC: U.S. *Government Printing Office*. In this 2010 brief on America's children, the Federal Interagency Forum on Child and Family Statistics reported that obesity levels among children ages 6 to 17 have been steadily rising since the mid-1970s. In 1976–80, only 6 percent of children ages 6 to 17 were obese. The percentage rose to 11 percent in 1988–94, to 17 percent in 2005–06, and to 19 percent by 2007–08.

7 Munoz K, et al. "Food Intakes of U.S. Children and Adolescents Compared with Recommendations." *Pediatrics* 1997; 100; 323-329.

8 Muntner, PhD, Paul, Jiang He, MD, PhD, Jeffrey A. Cutler, MD, Rachel P. Wildman, PhD, Paul K. Whelton, MD, MSc. " Trends in Blood Pressure Among Children and Adolescents." *JAMA* 2004; 291;2107–2113.

9 Ludwig, M.D., Ph.D., David S. "Childhood Obesity – The Shape of Things to Come." *N Engl J Med* 2007:357; 23.

10 Geier, Andrew B., Gary D. Foster, Leslie G. Womble, Jackie McLaughlin, Kelley E. Borradaile, Joan Nachmani, Sasha Sherman, Shiriki Kumanyika, and Justine Shults. "The Relationship between Relative Weight and School Attendance among Elementary Schoolchildren." *Obesity* 2007;15:2157–2161; Ludwig, M.D., Ph.D., David S. "Childhood Obesity – The Shape of Things to Come." *N Engl J Med* 2007:357;23.

11 Taras H, Potts-Datema W. "Obesity and Student Performance at School." *J School Health* 2005;75:291–295.

12 Christeson, William; Taggart, Amy Dawson and Messner-Zidell, Soren. "Too Fat to Fight; Retired Military Leaders Want Junk Food Out of America's Schools." *Mission: Readiness.* April 2010.

13 http://www.fns.usda.gov/FDD/processing/cp_faqs.htm

14 http://www.fns.usda.gov/fdd/processing/pfs-processing.pdf

15 http://www.fns.usda.gov/fdd/programs/schcnp/pfs-schcnp.pdf

16 Alaimo K., Olson C. M., Frongillo E. A. Jr. "Food Insufficiency and American School-Aged Children's Cognitive, Academic and Psychosocial Development." *Pediatrics* 2001;108(1): 44–53.

17 Wesnes K. A., Pincock C., Richardson D., Helm G., Hails S. "Breakfast reduces declines in attention and memory over the morning in schoolchildren." *Appetite* 2003;41(3):329–31. Benton D., Maconie A., Williams C. "The influence of the glycaemic load of breakfast on the behaviour of children in school." *Physiol Behav.* 2007 Nov 23;92(4):717–24. Epub 2007 May 31.

18 Rampersaud G. C., Pereira M. A., Girard B. L., Adams J., Metzl J. D. "Breakfast habits, nutritional status, body weight, and academic performance in children and adolescents." *J Am Diet Assoc.* 2005 May;105(5):743–60.

19 7 CFR §220.9(e). See http://www.fns.usda.gov/cnd/governance/Reauthorization_Policy_04/Reauthorization_04/2005-09-22.pdf for a detailed explanation.

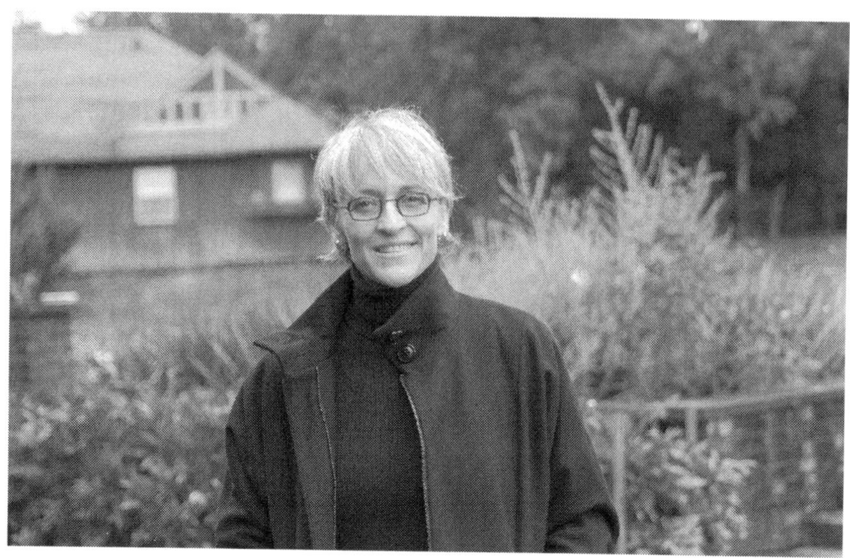

ABOUT THE AUTHOR

Kate Adamick is a food systems consultant and co-founder of *Cook for America®*, which provides concentrated and comprehensive culinary training to transform school food service personnel into skilled and passionate school *Lunch Teachers™*. Through both *Cook for America®* and her firm, *Food Systems Solutions® LLC*, Adamick has helped hundreds of schools throughout the United States transform their cafeterias into scratch-cooking operations.

Adamick, an attorney and classically trained professional chef, specializes in integrating operational changes, site-based programming, and public-private partnerships to create healthful institutional meal programs and to support local and sustainable agriculture systems. She has worked with school districts, hospitals, retirement communities, and foundations across the United States.

Adamick is a frequent speaker on institutional food systems, sustainable agriculture, childhood obesity issues, and the economics of school food reform.

Made in the USA
Charleston, SC
09 May 2012